Trackdown

THE SEARCH FOR THE MAD TRAPPER

Trackdown

THE SEARCH FOR THE MAD TRAPPER

BY THE AUTHOR OF
THE MAD TRAPPER OF RAT RIVER

DICK NORTH

To Rose
with best wishes
Dick North
Dawson City
Y.T.
Sept. 5, 1989

Macmillan of Canada
A Division of Canada Publishing Corporation
Toronto, Ontario, Canada

Canadian Cataloguing in Publication Data

North, Dick, date
Trackdown : the search for the mad trapper

Bibliography: p.
Includes index.
ISBN 0-7715-9209-4

1. Johnson, Albert, d. 1932.   2. Police murders –
Rat River Region (Yukon and N.W.T.).   3. Criminal
investigation – Rat River Region (Yukon and N.W.T.).
4. North, Dick.   I. Title.

FC4172.1.J6N67 1989   364.1'523'0924   C89-093407-X
F1060.9.J6N67 1989

Text and Jacket design: Don Fernley
Maps: Emma Hesse

MACMILLAN OF CANADA
A Division of Canada Publishing Corporation
Toronto, Ontario, Canada

Printed in Canada

For Andrée

ACKNOWLEDGEMENTS

THE LIST OF those who assisted on this work is a long one, and most of them are mentioned either in the text or in the appendix.

In addition, I would particularly like to express my appreciation to the Klondike Visitors' Association of Dawson City which graciously allowed me to devote time to this work at their Jack London Interpretive Center, where I am the Curator.

Thanks are also owed to the McNevin family, proprietors of the Eagle Plains Hotel which is located less than fifty miles from the scene of the final shootout between Johnson and the police. Much of the text was assembled at this Oasis-on-the-Tundra where I am known as "Writer-in-Residence".

I must also credit my late son Tim for his help in the early stages of research on the book.

Chris Tiller, retired RCMP superintendent, read the manuscript and offered valuable suggestions. These were mostly followed by this writer, and if any errors remain, they are mine. The same applies to material received from Superintendent Hoday of the RCMP.

Dick Hickman, CIB, and Editor of the North Dakota *Peace Officers Magazine* must be thanked for introducing me to Lena Stanley, a crucial source of primary material in my research.

Stan Horrall, RCMP historian, and Malcolm Wake, Director of the RCMP Museum in Regina, displayed their usual diligence in sending requested material to me.

Lastly, Sheldon Fischer, editor, should be credited with smoothing over the rough edges of the book through his candid observations and lucid insight.

The Arctic is a land of mystery. One of its greatest riddles has been the identity of Albert Johnson, "The Mad Trapper of Rat River". This is the story of my twenty-year search to find his roots.

CONTENTS

Author's Foreword *xi*
Prologue: The Manhunt *1*

Part One: Fifty Years of False Leads

1 The Early Clues: A Shortcut to Nowhere *16*
2 He Walked with a Stoop *32*
3 In the Wake of an Elusive Scandinavian *41*
4 Bill Johnson and the Black Lake Mystery *55*
5 The Ex-Cop Hypothesis and Another Cold Trail *64*
6 The Mysterious Disappearance of Zane Grey's Guide *73*
7 The Eccentric Carpenter from Anyox *78*
8 The "Wrong Man" Theme *84*

Part Two: A Northern Legacy of the Wild West

9 The Badlands Immigrants *92*
10 On the Trail of a Wyoming Horse Thief *103*
11 The Road to Folsom Prison *116*
12 Fingerprints: Let the Sleeping Dog Lie *124*
13 The Net Tightens *149*
14 Another Run at Exhumation *160*
Epilogue *174*

Endnotes *179*
Appendix A – Personal Effects of Albert Johnson *183*
Appendix B – Vital Statistics and Modus Operandi *185*
Appendix C – Sources *194*

Index *197*

LIST OF PHOTOGRAPHS,
DOCUMENTS AND MAPS

On or following page

x. Death photo of Albert Johnson
3. Abe Francis
5. "Mad Trapper's" cabin on Rat River
14. Map: Yukon Territory and northern British Columbia
17. Inspector A. N. Eames
26. RCMP artist's portrait of "Mad Trapper"
27. Identikit portrait of "Mad Trapper"
35. "Arthur Nelson" at Ross River
46. Letter from Robert Alexie, with typescript
53. *Dawson News* clipping re Lingle murder
58. Trapper Bill Johnson
66. Harry Johnson
69. Idaho murderer Bill Banty
76. Guide and prospector Sivert Nielson
87. Yukon trapper Phil Branstrom
90. Map: Montana, Wyoming and North Dakota
94. Baptismal certificate of Johnny Johnson
101. Medicine Lake, Montana
105. *Medicine Lake Wave* clipping re bank robbery
110. Criminal warrant for "William Hoffner"
118. *Lassen County News* clipping re "Charles W. Johnson"
122. Folsom Prison
125. Johnny Johnson mug shot, Lincoln County Jail
126. Johnny Johnson mug shot, Wyoming State Penitentiary
128. Johnny Johnson mug shot, San Quentin
134. Letter from Coroner R. L. James
140. Julian Folvag letter
143. Letter from Wyoming State Penitentiary
144. Typical specimens for fingerprint patterns
147. Johnny Johnson's fingerprints
151. Letter from Tom Smith
157. Lena Stanley
158. Johnny Johnson's Draft Registration
169. Comparison of photographic profiles
170. Close-up of Johnny Johnson showing facial anomalies
171. Close-up of "Albert Johnson" showing facial anomalies
173. Wyoming State Penitentiary Registration form
176. Leo Brothers

AUTHOR'S FOREWORD

T HE MASS OF GELID AIR enfolded the isolated blubber shed at Aklavik, Northwest Territories, like an invisible shroud. Its icy tentacles bound a man suspended from a beam by a rope under his arms. He hung awkwardly, at an angle, his features locked in a macabre grimace accentuated by wide-open stoic blue eyes that could not see, frostbitten ears that could not hear, a nose swollen so bulbously that it looked like that of a clown, and purple-tinged lips silenced forever by the permanence of death. His face was framed by an ice-encrusted beard disguising a less-than-firm chin that belied the steely will of the man he had been. If one moved closer and rudely removed the tarp that was wrapped around him, one would see that the frozen corpse was rent with seven bullet holes, mute testimony to the fact that the death of the man called Albert Johnson had not been a tranquil one. . . .

The scene shifts to far-off Bolivia twenty-three years earlier in 1909. Soldiers stare at a man lying before them, dead by his own hand from his last bullet after fighting off a detachment of the Bolivian army in an all-night gun battle. The body lies there looking oddly peaceful, eyes staring vacantly at the nearby peaks of the Andes Mountains. Several feet away lies the crumpled figure of his companion shot through with rifle bullets and just as still.

An officer barks a command in Spanish and the bodies are toted away. He is overheard saying that the dead men are two

Albert Johnson in death, February 18, 1932. The photograph was taken from an awkwardly low position. RCMP ARCHIVES

American desperados, Butch Cassidy and Harry Longabaugh, the "Sundance Kid", of the Wild Bunch. . . .

The tableau switches yet again, to an underpass on one of Chicago's busiest main streets in 1930. A reporter for the Chicago *Tribune* is quietly approached from behind and suddenly gunned down by a blond-haired man with a handgun. The slaying becomes one of the most publicized events in the criminal history of the Windy City. Even after a man is brought to trial and convicted of the deed, the suspicion lingers that the convicted man was innocent: who killed Jake Lingle, then, and why? . . .

My adventures in seeking out the roots of Albert Johnson were akin to those of the prospector who once looked for a stray burro and found a mountain of silver. In my case, however, the discoveries were historical anomalies rather than motherlodes of precious metals.

In the course of my metaphorical digging, I not only produced the aforementioned threads connecting Johnson's saga to the "Wild West" and to Chicago, but also found a policeman who once served time as a prisoner in the notorious Alcatraz prison and who was the probable origin of the Johnson-was-an-ex-cop idea; uncovered the Mexican hideaway of writer Zane Grey's Norwegian guide who disappeared in 1924; elicited the vague destination of a murderer, thought to be Johnson, who escaped the clutches of the law in the state of Idaho; unravelled a riddle thought to involve the "Mad Trapper" that implied foul play in the odd death of a hermit on the shores of Black Lake in northern Saskatchewan in the early twenties; exploded a theory suggesting that the RCMP gunned down the wrong man; and—lastly—found the roots of Albert Johnson, "The Man from Nowhere".

PROLOGUE:

THE MANHUNT

ALBERT JOHNSON, blond, ruggedly built, appeared at Fort McPherson, Northwest Territories, on July 9, 1931, after floating down the Peel River on a three-log raft. He pitched camp on the spruce-studded river bank about a mile above the community. Johnson was a quiet man, not given to idle conversation and generally unsociable. However, he was not reluctant to demonstrate his ability with a short gun, and one day he put on a shooting exhibition near his camp the likes of which had never been seen before in that town, and probably will never be seen again.

Aware that there were witnesses, he methodically paced off an impressive target distance and set up two three-foot sticks in the sand, and "with a pistol in each hand shot the top off of each stick, crossed hands and shot again."[1] He continued to repeat this eye-opening performance, and according to Indians who saw him whittled about one inch off the tops of the sticks with each phenomenal fusillade.

Word of this mastery of shooting irons spread like wildfire over the surprisingly efficient "moccasin telegraph" and in a short time became part and parcel of the legend of Albert Johnson. Indeed, this was probably the stranger's intent. If one wanted to ensure isolation, there would be no better way to do so than by demonstrating an infallible accuracy with firearms. The reason for this was probably to discourage prying eyes that might see he had approximately $3,400 in cash in his possession.

In addition, since we know the weapons found on Johnson when he was killed included a .22 rifle with the stock sawed off and a 16-gauge shotgun with the barrel cut down and part of the stock removed, he may have been practising to check the weapons' balance and his own capabilities with them. He may also have borrowed revolvers from someone, since no revolvers were ever found among his possessions. To this date, there are still some unanswered questions about the exact weapons he used during his time at Fort McPherson, but there is no question at all about his skills, which apparently were unparalleled.

Again, Johnson did not go unnoticed when he purchased goods at the two local trading posts. He would purchase an article and pay for it with a large bill and pocket the change. Then he would walk around and look and buy something else, paying for each item as he obtained it, and always with bills removed from different pockets. This was a habit of some practicality. An individual who was leery of displaying a large bankroll might proceed in this manner.

The newcomer stayed in the vicinity of Fort McPherson for two weeks and during that time had little discourse with anyone other than storekeepers, and Abe Francis, who lived across the river from his camp and eventually sold him a small canoe. Altogether, this man, who gave his name as Albert Johnson, spent about $1,000 in putting together a trail outfit while at McPherson.

And Johnson also exhibited a gentler side of his personality. On one occasion after buying the 16-gauge shotgun—the same one that was found in his possession after he was killed—he told the manager of the Hudson's Bay post to put the change toward distributing free candy among the many youngsters who frequented the premises.[2]

Another time, when John Robert, clerk of the Northern Trader's store, tried to sell him an outboard motor for the canoe Johnson had just purchased from Francis, he refused, flexing his arms with good humour and telling Robert that *they* were good enough motor power for him.

But except for those rare incidents, the stranger kept to

Abe Francis packing supplies up Stony Creek, over Chute Pass to La Pierre House, 1929. Johnson camped across the Peel River from Francis in the summer of 1931. AMOS BURG

himself, pending a journey back into the bush.

RCMP Constable Edgar Millen talked briefly with Johnson near the end of July. He asked the stranger where he spent the winter. Johnson said he had "been working on the prairies last summer and winter [1930–1931] and had come into the country by way of the Mackenzie River."[3]

This did not jibe with Millen's knowledge that the stranger had come down the Peel and had asked Indians he had passed if he was on the Porcupine River. The source of the Porcupine was far to the west and no man who had floated down the Mackenzie River to the east would have confused the two rivers and made such a query.

Johnson was not clear on his plans for the future, but did say he might go west to the Yukon Territory. Millen advised him that if he did decide to trap on the McPherson side of the mountains he would have to buy a Northwest Territories' licence. This Johnson refused to do.

Contrary to what he told the Mountie, Johnson did not go to the Yukon Territory. On July 21 he set out down the Peel River and passed Arthur Blake's post, then returned and asked Blake how to get to the Rat River. Blake recommended one way but also mentioned another, more difficult route which he did not recommend. Johnson took the tougher route and in August built a cabin on the Rat River less than fifty miles northwest of Fort McPherson. While there he tolerated no visitors, and associated with no one. Those who passed his cabin were leery of his presence. Four months later, in December, an Indian from the area named William Nerysoo complained that Johnson was tampering with his traps and trapping without a licence.

Constable Alfred King was dispatched from the nearest RCMP post at Arctic Red River to interview the hermit and to check him out. King and his Indian interpreter, Joe Bernard, arrived at Johnson's cabin after a two-day trip and espied the loner peeking at them from behind a burlap tarp that covered the window. Johnson quickly flipped down the sack when he saw the two men looking back at him.

Speaking loudly to be sure Johnson could hear him through the walls of the solidly built dwelling, King said that he wanted to talk with him about the neighbour's complaint. But the loner would not respond or acknowledge the Mountie's remarks in any way. King repeated his appeal several times, then warned Johnson that he would have to get a search warrant if he did not

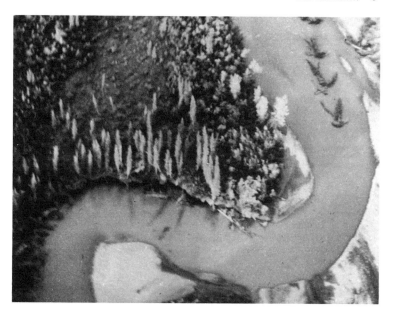

Albert Johnson's cabin on the Rat River was situated across from
the sand spit at bottom left. (River flows from left to right.)
BOB CAMERON

cooperate. Johnson still would not answer, so King and Bernard mushed their dog teams to the Sub-District Headquarters
in Aklavik for further instructions.

The commander, Inspector A. N. Eames, issued a warrant
and sent King and his special constable back to Rat River with
reinforcements in the person of another constable and his
guide. They got there on the thirty-first. Eames had told King to
break down the door to the hermit's shack if he found it necessary to do so. As it turned out, the constable never had the
chance. Johnson shot as soon as King knocked, the bullet
splintering the door to pierce the Mountie's chest. The force of
the slug bowled King over into the snow. Bleeding profusely
from a lung wound, he managed to crawl to the riverbank under
covering fire from the others. He was immediately placed on a

sled and the four raced against time back to Aklavik. In the process, King's bedroll, which had been removed to make room for him, was forgotten. Johnson later appropriated it for his own use.

The shooting of King inspired prompt action on the part of Inspector Eames and he organized a posse, but unlike the "wild west" of warmer climes, where a man could grab a sandwich, canteen, packroll and head out on his horse in a matter of minutes, it took days to put a constabulary afield in the Arctic in mid-winter. The crux of the problem was the need for food for the dog teams. This consisted primarily of fish gathered by trappers in the summer. It took many hours of work to accumulate a winter's supply, and dog mushers were reluctant to part with it. Without such "fuel" though, transport was not easy to come by in the Arctic.

It took Eames five days to muster his forces and supplies for chasing Johnson, and it took four more for the Inspector and his men to mush to the cabin of the cranky misanthrope on the Rat River. Eames and his men presumed Johnson would have fled the area during the interval from December 31, 1931 to January 9, 1932, but surprisingly Johnson had stayed put, perhaps waiting to flee in a snowstorm that would obliterate his tracks.

After making sure his men were safely in position below the riverbank twenty meters from the cabin, Eames shouted to Johnson that King had not died, and if he surrendered he could expect leniency on the part of the law. The answer was stony silence.

Inspector Eames ordered his men to fire on the cabin and sent several forays against it, but Johnson's counterfire kept them at bay. Ultimately, after nine hours of futile shooting, dynamite was hurled at the structure and under cover of the blast several men rushed the redoubt. A trapper, Knut Lang, who had been deputized by Inspector Eames, managed to break down part of the door only to see Johnson trying to get a bead on him with "two handguns" from under his bunk. Lang said the man appeared stunned from the blast which did little actual damage, but when he recovered his senses and started firing, Lang ducked out of sight and withdrew to the safety of the riverbank.

The fight settled into a standoff, and after fifteen hours, Eames called off the posse, claiming a lack of supplies as his chief reason. There was also a more practical reason. During one of the sorties, a flashlight had been attached to a stick by a member of the posse and its beam directed inside the cabin. No sooner had the light been flicked on than Johnson, in a lightning reflex response, put it out with one shot. The men later examined the flashlight and found a hole through the bulb housing, probably made by a .22 bullet.

The hermit's unerring aim had a sobering effect on the small siege party for it substantiated rumours that had circulated about Johnson's unbelievable show of trick shooting at McPherson. Eames did not want to risk the loss of any of his men through impatience or reckless efforts to end the confrontation.

Leaving two men to watch the shack, Eames and his party returned to Aklavik. He wired A. C. Acland, Superintendent of "G" Division in Edmonton, Alberta, explaining what had happened and added the following:

> MILLEN HAD CONVERSATION WITH JOHNSON LAST JULY AND DESCRIBES HIM AS 5'8". FAIR HAIR. LIGHT BLUE EYES. SLIGHT SCANDINAVIAN ACCENT. INCLINED TO STOOP.

Eames realized that, until he could muster more supplies, he would have to maintain a smaller party that would try to flush out the fugitive. Once that was accomplished he could move in a larger party to either capture or kill Johnson.

Eames sent four men, led by Constable Millen, back down the well-worn trail to the Rat River. They reached Johnson's shack to learn from the two men left there that the recluse had taken advantage of a fierce blizzard to make his getaway.

They examined the cabin which proved to be staunchly constructed. The frame consisted of a double row of sill logs and a dirt floor countersunk about two feet below the surface of the ground. Johnson's bunk was made of full logs with yet a second lower tier excavated beneath it. This had served him as a pill-box type of refuge into which he scurried when the men started to break down the door. One of the reasons he had not shot Lang was that he could not immediately bring his weapons to bear from beneath his bunk because of the awkward angle down under the logs.

It was obvious to Millen and the others with him that Johnson was not only a good man with an axe, but a master wood craftsman as well. Testimony to this was a pair of snowshoe frames the men found hanging on the wall. The snowshoes' frames were a hefty three inches thick and double webbed in the middle—different from the usual shoe, so they would leave an easy track to recognize and follow. Though crude, they were more than adequate for their purpose and exemplified good workmanship, considering Johnson possessed only such implements as a knife fashioned from a spring trap, a three-cornered file, an awl made from a piece of the file, an axe with a hand-hewn handle, and a chisel shaped from a nail.

Millen and his three companions figured Johnson had probably headed up the Rat to get away from the more populated areas in the delta of the Peel and Mackenzie Rivers rather than downstream. They set off in the direction of the Richardson Mountains to the west and picked up Johnson's trail on a tributary far up the Rat River. After sixteen gruelling days, they managed to corner him in a small canyon. In the gun battle that ensued, Constable Millen was killed. Johnson managed to work his way up a steep cliff and escape.

Inspector Eames, on learning of this reverse and now recognizing the desperate nature and skill of the man he was tracking, wired his commander in Edmonton and requested a plane. He needed the aircraft to bring supplies as well as to scout out Johnson's trail. He also sought the services of another Mountie to replace Millen. Via an Anchorage, Alaska, radio station he announced that he was setting up a base camp at the mouth of the Rat River and he appealed to every able-bodied man in the vicinity to go there with plenty of ammunition and supplies.

The pressure was mounting on Eames. If he was not quickly successful he knew he would become the laughing stock of the Arctic. Johnson, alone, on foot, and unable even to hunt (lest rifle shots give his position away), was running circles around the Mounties with all their dog-teams, Indian guides and sleds full of supplies. Lurid stories about Johnson's skills had made headlines throughout North America and even Europe. After sending out the various messages, Eames set out again for Rat River.

In response to Eames' request, Superintendent Acland advised him by wireless that the plane and services of another Mountie had been approved and would be dispatched north in a few days. He concluded the wire with a blunt order:

TAKE ALBERT JOHNSON'S FINGERPRINTS AFTER CAPTURE WHETHER DEAD OR NOT AND FORWARD HERE QUICKEST METHOD.

This first reference to fingerprints underscored the importance attached to them. Clearly, the RCMP felt the clue to the mystery man lay in his prints. It would be nothing short of unprofessional not to take them if the opportunity presented itself.

Meanwhile, Corporal Arthur B. Thornthwaite, NCO-in-Charge of the Old Crow, Yukon Territory detachment, whose jurisdiction was immediately across the Richardson Mountains from the scene of the manhunt, heard the inspector's plea and, on January 21, dispatched his one constable, Sid May, and Special Constable John Moses to join Eames' search party. May put together a small posse of his own and then mushed across Rat Pass to join the larger group.

The pursuit of Johnson was in full cry. The request for a plane had been honoured and the aircraft winged its way northward under the capable guidance of pilot "Wop" May (no relation to Const. May). With him was Constable William Carter, the RCMP officer selected to replace Millen. Also in the plane was the mechanic, Jack Bowen. They landed at Aklavik, refueled and then were delayed by bad weather.

The following day they flew to the Rat and, after first flying a reconnaissance of the upper Rat and Barrier Rivers, May landed at the main camp and let off Constable Carter. Valuable dog food was unloaded at the same time and dispersed among the many waiting dog teams.

The next day Carter joined Constable Sid May and his group who headed on foot up the Barrier River in search of the trapper. The tributary's source was an area that drained one of the highest saddles in the Richardson Mountains. After a hard day on the trail in weather that was clear but extremely cold, the men were about to return to camp when John Moses spotted Johnson's peculiar snowshoe print. The Indian, who was an experienced tracker, did not think at first that Johnson would attempt to cross the Richardsons. But when he picked up this faint print, he pointed to the source of the Barrier and remarked, "Look, that man go this way. He wait for big wind, when he go over, snow is hard—no trail—no catch 'em quick."[4]

At that latitude, above the Arctic Circle, the mountains are barren and windswept and, worst of all, treeless. Anyone attempting to cross them at that time of year would have to pack along a personal supply of firewood.

Moses observed that no Indian would even think of making such a trip unless it were a last resort. In Johnson's case, of course, it was just that, a last bid for freedom. He traversed the range in a raging blizzard, during which time he either lost or discarded his bedroll because he was becoming too weak to carry it. Also, if indeed he did have in his possession two revolvers as rumoured, this would have been the point and place where they were discarded. They would only have been a hindrance to the fugitive since their range was too short to be used effectively against men with rifles in open country.

Moses and, later, Peter Alexie, a trapper who had just crossed the mountains, reported that Johnson's tracks had been spotted on the western side of the Richardsons that night. Accordingly, Eames made plans to move the search to the other side of the range. Eames, Carter and several other men flew across the divide with pilot Wop May and set up camp at the Jackson brothers' trading post at La Pierre House. Sid May and his group again mushed their dogs across the pass at the head-waters of Rat River to join Inspector Eames.

A few days later, on February 17, 1932, after Wop May had spotted Johnson's snowshoe tracks from the air, the posse ran head on into the fugitive twenty-five miles up the Eagle River from its junction with the Bell. Johnson put Royal Canadian Signals Sergeant Earl Hersey out of action with an intuitive shot that sent a bullet through his knee, elbow, and chest, causing five wounds with one slug. Hersey had been in a kneeling position shooting at Johnson when he was hit.

The posse quickly surrounded the desperate man in the middle of the frozen river by taking to the riverbanks on both sides of Johnson. This manoeuvre put them thirty feet above the fugitive. Eames shouted for Johnson to surrender, but the man's only reply was an undecipherable wave of the hand, followed by the blast of his rifle.

One of the men on the bank immediately above Johnson was Special Constable John Moses. In an interview later, he recalled that he had barely peeked over the bank at Johnson when the desperado noticed the movement out of the corner of his eye and immediately directed his aim from the others to Moses. The latter aimed his gun at Johnson and fired. The trapper did not shoot back, possibly because he was hit with Moses's shot, but more likely because a fusillade from the posse hit him simultaneously.[5]

The men who faced Johnson were crack shots: seven bullets hit him, and since only seven men were close enough to get a bearing on him at that time, it indicates that not one of them missed the target.

Johnson lay prostrate, his head face down in the snow. The posse ceased fire, and after waiting ten minutes the men gingerly approached him. Finally, Constable Sid May turned the man over and saw that his face was a rigidly frozen death mask. The Mad Trapper of Rat River would shoot no more.

Not even a cursory check was made of Johnson's effects at that time because of a mammoth dogfight that broke out among the unattended animals while the shootout was in progress. The posse turned their attention to breaking that up while several of the men attended to Sergeant Hersey, who was quickly loaded onto Wop May's plane for the flight to Aklavik that saved his life.

Once these details were settled, some heed was paid to Johnson, whose body was lifted and placed on a sled by Constable May. Sid found the body surprisingly light and doubted if he weighed "much over one hundred pounds, he was so emaciated."[6]

Albert Johnson's body was taken by Joe Verville, one of the trappers deputized into the posse, and his dog team to La Pierre House. During the trip the sled rolled over several times and the corpse suffered rough treatment while negotiating steep banks of the river on the portages. This may have caused some damage to Johnson's features, of which no photo had yet been taken.

Once the men reached La Pierre House, Johnson's body was wrapped in a tarp and shoved feet-first into a log-pole cache atop a fifteen-foot-high platform next to the Jackson brothers' trading post. There it was safe for the night from any marauding predators.

The next day Wop May flew in and landed at the makeshift landing strip tamped down by the snowshoe-shod men of the posse. The body was loaded onto the plane and Inspector Eames climbed aboard for the flight to headquarters. A few hours later May landed the plane at Aklavik.

The manhunt that had lasted forty-five days, and elicited superhuman behaviour that has seldom been matched in the annals of Arctic life, was over. But now Eames was faced with a problem that would take even longer—indeed, half a century—to solve: the problem of finding out the identity of the strange man his posse had gunned down.

PART ONE

FIFTY YEARS
OF FALSE
LEADS

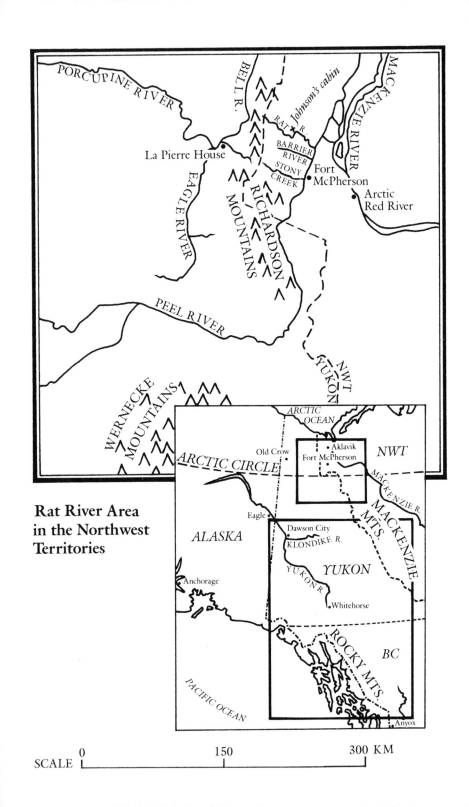

PORCUPINE RIVER

BELL R.

Johnson's cabin

RAT R.

MACKENZIE RIVER

La Pierre House

BARRIER RIVER

STONY CREEK

Fort McPherson

Arctic Red River

EAGLE RIVER

RICHARDSON MOUNTAINS

PEEL RIVER

NWT

YUKON

WERNECKE MOUNTAINS

Rat River Area in the Northwest Territories

ARCTIC OCEAN

Old Crow

Aklavik
Fort McPherson

NWT

ARCTIC CIRCLE

MACKENZIE R.

Eagle

MACKENZIE MTS.

ALASKA

Dawson City
KLONDIKE R.

YUKON

YUKON R.

Anchorage

Whitehorse

ROCKY MTS.

BC

PACIFIC OCEAN

Anyox

SCALE
0   150   300 KM

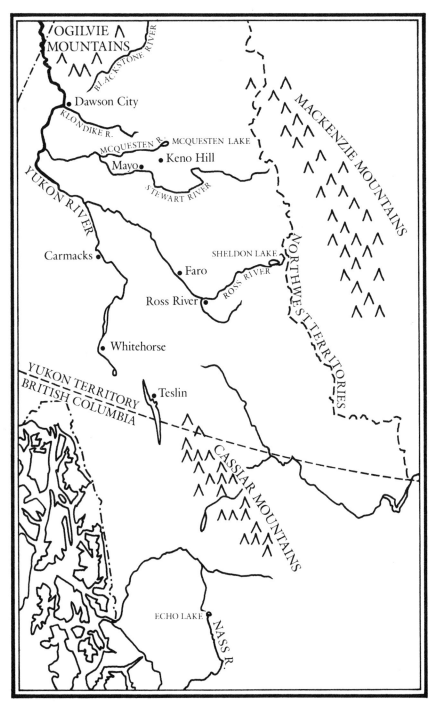

Johnson's Sojourn Northward

SCALE 0 ____ 150 KM

CHAPTER 1

THE EARLY CLUES:
A SHORTCUT TO NOWHERE

THE GREATEST MANHUNT in the history of the Royal Canadian Mounted Police ended with the unidentified body they had flown in from Eagle River unceremoniously stowed in a blubber shed behind the detachment station at Aklavik, Northwest Territories. The Mounties had "got their man", tentatively called Albert Johnson, but who was he?

On February 18, 1932, Inspector Alexander N. Eames, who directed the manhunt, initiated procedures to find out. No papers or identification had been found either in Johnson's cabin or on his body. Thus, first priority was the fingerprints. Eames painstakingly lifted these from the dead man's frozen hands. Next he photographed Johnson, then requested that the resident physician draw up a physical description of him. The prints, photos, and the profile were placed in a dispatch bag and sent out by plane to headquarters in Ottawa three days later.

For many months thereafter, Inspector Eames responded to scores of letters sent to him by people who figured Albert Johnson might be someone they knew.

The first note was not long in coming. It was dated the same day Johnson was killed. A Minook, Alberta, man wrote to say that a neighbour of his by the name of John Sylvester Stepan had deserted his wife five years earlier. The man was a blacksmith by trade, and good in the bush. Stepan's wife had implored the neighbour to write to the Mounties on her behalf. Later a solicitor mailed a photograph of the blacksmith to the RCMP, and Stepan was quickly ruled out as being Johnson because

Inspector A. N. Eames, who later rose to the rank of Assistant Commissioner. RCMP ARCHIVES

there was not the least resemblance between the two men.

The next query came from within the RCMP themselves. The Commander of "G" Division mentioned that an inspector in Aklavik, S. T. Wood, had mentioned a man named Johnson in a report in 1922. The man had arrived in Fort McPherson in a canvas boat with his clothes in rags and no food. He remained a few days and then left for the Yukon. Eames traced this yarn and learned from the recollections of Peter Alexie, a trapper, that the ragged man had been known as "Deep Hole" Johnson and was not the Albert they had killed.

Wood also had reported that two men had ventured into the delta of the Mackenzie in 1922 and had "spread poison baits wholesale and sprung traps of the Eskimo". One of them, Victor Petersen, was convicted of the poison offence, and both were shipped out of the country. The funds that had accrued from the sale of the offenders' confiscated furs were used to speed the men on their way. (The name of the second man was not included in the reference.)

Wood added in his 1922 report that there was a growing number of "intruders" who tended to be either unprepared for the country or unwilling to abide by its trapping laws. His comments proved to be an accurate forecast of what would happen in later years as the Depression forced desperate men off their farms and out of the cities, and provided a context in which anonymous men like Albert Johnson wandered, restless and rootless.

Local rumours among the natives suggested that Albert Johnson may have really been John Brown, who had left the Old Crow district in 1928. Eames dismissed the John Brown rumour easily, for he himself had committed Brown to an asylum after he went insane at Coppermine, Northwest Territories, in 1930. Brown's real name was Barkauckas and he was a Russian.

RCMP files show a great many other enquiries, including many from the United States, and one from Henry Holm, the vice consul of Finland. All of them were dismissed for one reason or another. A rumour that persisted for many years was that the Mad Trapper was Albert F. Johnson of Troy, Montana, who had participated in an archeological dig in China during the 1920s. This rumour was dispelled only recently when I ascertained that he died in 1956 in the Lincoln County Rest

Home in Libby, Montana, at the age of eighty-one, in 1956.

One letter seems more pertinent but it was not retained or has been lost. In it, a J. M. Taylor, of Nation, Alaska, wrote of an individual who had been in that area. Eames wrote the following to the Commanding Officer of "G" Division in Edmonton: "The habits, actions and demeanour of the man described in Mr. Taylor's letter conform in some respects to those exhibited by Albert Johnson. To the late Constable Millen and others at McPherson, N.W.T., last July, Albert Johnson appeared to be quite rational."

Another which proved to be of interest was a note from Joe F. Krom of the Kromona Mining and Smelting Company of Spokane, Washington. Dated October 14, 1932, the letter mentioned that a man he had known in the army at Fort Lewis, Washington, had corresponded with him from the North and used the alias "Albert Johnson . . . . for reasons of his own". Krom added he would give the RCMP this man's real name if they felt the lead were worth checking out. There is no record of this having been followed up.

Letters continued to come, even after Eames had left the Arctic. One was written by an R. J. Gill of the American Dredging Company in Oakland, California, in 1938. Gill stated that he had met a man up north in 1925 whom he thought could be Albert Johnson, and who looked very much like the death photo published in a detective magazine that he enclosed with the letter. Gill said he always thought the individual he had known was a little "cracked". He described the man as five foot eleven, with grey eyes, blond hair, who weighed about two hundred pounds. He said the man was ungainly in build with "funny looking teeth, two were very small on the left side of the upper mouth that seemed to grow out of the gum above the others." Gill said he smoked a pipe and was a good shot. He added that someone had told him that this man had once been a Mountie "so you should know if this is so."[1]

Gill said he was writing the letter on behalf of three sisters of the individual. The RCMP replied that the three sisters Gill was representing should supply them with all the details plus a photo and they would attempt to identify him. This lead was never followed up either.

The failure of correspondence to turn up any significant information about the identity of Albert Johnson was reflected in the Mounties' own efforts. The Identification Section of the RCMP examined and circulated Eames' own information and the photos but, with the exception of a single lead in the Yukon Territory, came up with no clue to the riddle of Albert Johnson's roots. The mystery remained unsolved for more than thirty years, and gradually entered the realm of legend.

I came on the scene much later. I was a reporter, and in the winter of 1963-64 was sent to cover the inaugural winter opening of the Haines Junction lateral of the Alaska Highway. I had barely stepped across the border into the Yukon Territory before I heard of Johnson and the incredible Arctic battle which had pitted him against one of the world's great police forces.

In the evening a cinematographer friend, Chuck Keen, and I headed for the bar at the hotel where we were staying. Chuck had dislocated one of his vertebrae while filming, and I had accompanied him back to Whitehorse. Fortunately, we picked a hostelry owned by Cal Miller, a gigantic, cigar-chomping proprietor who had turned his inn, which he called the Capital Hotel, into a second home for prospectors, miners, trappers, cowboys, hunters, big game outfitters, and construction men from miles around.

At that time the Yukon Territory was engaged in one of the greatest staking rushes in her young history. The Faro group of mining claims which was found to cover millions of tons of lead and zinc was a magnet that drew prospectors from all over North America. Everyone wanted to carve out a piece of the pie for himself, and as a result local hotels were bursting at the seams.

When you walk into a place you have never been before, you seldom forget your first impressions. Mine was of Miller—a rotund, brash, and impatient man—who was in deep conversation with a prospector who wore the classic white, army-type muklucks of nylon tops and rubber soles and an open parka with a tuque placed jauntily on his head.

"Yeah," I heard Cal say, "I got you about the anomaly [trace of mineralization], but you haven't told me how much of a stake you want."

I could not hear what the man answered as his back was to me, but Cal Miller nonchalantly pulled a bankroll from his pocket, peeled off five one-hundred-dollar bills, and asked: "Is that enough jawbone?"

The man nodded his thanks, took the funds, and walked off.

Under that gruff exterior of his, Miller was basically a generous man who understood the psyche of his customers, and catered to it, and that is one of the reasons why the men piled into his saloon. He invited us to join him and a colourful group of eight or more men clustered around two tables pushed together.

I recall some of them: Al Kulan, grey hair, slight of build, who with Ross River Indians Arthur John, Joe and Jack Ladue and others had found the fabulous ore zone that triggered the staking rush; and Barry O'Neil, of the Keno City area, who once mined a pocket of silver ore that ran 680 ounces to the ton, and prospected the Wernecke Mountains with guide Lonnie Johnny. The latter, who could live on the proverbial snare wire and a match for six months alone in the bush, was later to freeze to death in downtown Mayo, rendered helpless by too much liquor. Pete Jenson was there, a former Mountie who was now an outfitter on the Dempster Highway, and whose guide, Robert Martin, one winter drove a dog team from Mayo to Aklavik, a distance of five hundred miles across one of the wildest, most uninhabited stretches of North America, just to see his girlfriend (whom he later married).

Another man present was Alex Van Bibber, of the formidable Van Bibber clan, half Indian, half "West Virginian", who once guided a surveyor for the proposed Canol pipeline three hundred miles up the Stewart River to cross the backbone of the continent, the Mackenzie Mountains, by dog team with temperatures ranging down to 75°(F) below zero.

It wasn't long before the yarns poured forth in staccato bursts like the drone of a machine gun, and one wondered where the truth ended and the fibbing began. As the spirits took effect and tongues loosened, talk wandered to the subject of Albert Johnson, a man whom they said shot a Mountie and fled after an all-night gun battle.

My companions, all of whom had lived outside when the mercury was extremely low, described the stamina of this man (of whom I then knew nothing), who, while on the run, survived brutal minus sixty temperatures without even a tent for several weeks. They exalted this loner, whom they called "The Mad Trapper", and they boasted of his ability on the trail as if he were a friend or relative rather than a man who had transgressed the law. To them he was something of a hero. And even a scattering of Mounties in the same crowd talked of him as warriors will extoll the brave deeds of a fallen foe.

These men had tramped the barrens and knew what *real* cold was. They had seen diesel fuel turn to slush at 70 below zero, and propane tanks stop flowing because the cold has liquified the gas. They had seen inversions typical of the north when temperatures in the river bottoms could read 75 below and five hundred feet above be a comparatively balmy minus 55.

These men knew what cold could do to inanimate objects and they knew what it could do to a man. One false step—one unthinking act—one moment of carelessness, and the encompassing cold could kill surprisingly quickly.

Exposure of flesh at minus seventy will freeze the skin in thirty seconds! Such cold can render ungloved hands immovable in the same amount of time, and cripple a man with wet feet almost as fast. Those unaccustomed to real cold and camping out can wake up to find their toothpaste as solid as a rock, eggs frozen like stones, and a can of fruit as hard as a sledgehammer. Unlike unbearable heat, for which there is usually some sanctuary of shade, cold allows no such refuge. Only fire can provide an external source of relief, and without the ability and materials to make a fire, a human being is virtually doomed in the wilderness at such low temperatures.

Thus, those who knew, commented on the sheer guts of the man known as Albert Johnson, and his ability to function when he dared not light a fire at minus sixty, and on his ability to fight when he had no food to stoke a body that must have cried out for sustenance to fuel internal warmth. They relived the final minutes when Johnson exchanged shot for shot until the unerring aim of the experienced woodsmen of the posse brought him down like a hunted animal.

This conversation, the bits and pieces of which I had picked up during the course of the night, piqued my curiosity about Albert Johnson, particularly when the sourdoughs commented that he was an unknown, a mystery man, who had never been identified by the RCMP or anyone else. They hashed and rehashed rumours that Johnson was an American bank robber; an ex-Mountie gone wrong; a Russian spy wandering through the Arctic; a bushed Scandinavian prospector; and so on until claims and staking again took over the conversation.

The next day I was preoccupied with churning out newspaper copy on the Haines Road opening. I shoved thoughts of the Mad Trapper onto the back burner and went about my business.

My next chance to take a look at the Johnson legend came when I took a canoe trip down the Yukon River in 1964 and again six months later when I undertook a dog sled journey in the Territory. I made my permanent home in Whitehorse beginning in August, 1966, and became privy to enough previously unknown information about Johnson to write a book about him, which included as much as was known at that time.[2] But while pursuing that task, I decided to continue my research with the idea that someday I might at last be able to identify him.

In order to accomplish this goal, I settled on an elementary procedure: I would establish both a detailed psychological and physical profile of Albert Johnson, and then find a man to fit them.

My task was made simpler by the dossier Eames had compiled as well as the reservoir of facts that I myself had gathered on Johnson. First, I wrote down his modus operandi, or all his habits and idiosyncracies, based on what was known about him from the time he arrived at Fort McPherson to his death on the Eagle River eight months later.

According to Constable Millen, Albert Johnson spoke with a slight Scandinavian accent, suggesting that he was either an immigrant from Norway, Denmark, or Sweden, or raised by immigrant parents in North America.

He was a loner and obviously an outdoor man.

When Johnson was killed he carried no identification of any sort on his person. Though this was not entirely unprecedented behaviour, usually even the most reclusive trapper preserved some dog-eared memento of family or friends. The total absence of any letter or photo in his cabin as well suggests that Johnson may have deliberately avoided carrying such items. This intentional anonymity, then, would have some significance if found to be true of the habits of a similar individual who had been known elsewhere.

There seemed to be a consensus among the residents of Fort McPherson that "Albert Johnson" was an alias.[3] Trappers like Paul Nieman, Constable Millen, and the Anglican missionary Reverend Geddes all were dubious. If he used one, he could have used more, and that would be of import.

Johnson demonstrated a propensity to lie when he felt the occasion demanded it, as he did to Millen when he said he came down the Mackenzie River.

According to the original complainant, Johnson was a thief, robbing trap lines and interfering with them.

Another intriguing habit of Johnson's emerged from the recollections of the officers and trappers who had spent weeks tracking him. They remarked that their quarry, like a moose, frequently doubled back when pursued. This proclivity suggested that he may have been chased more than once.

Albert Johnson before and during the manhunt demonstrated so phenomenal an ability with firearms that this skill almost certainly would have been recognized wherever he had previously lived.

Furthermore, the trapper was an excellent craftsman of wood and had probably at one time or another worked with metal. This is demonstrated by his creditable job of cutting down the barrel of his shotgun.

His clothes were nondescript. At his death he was wearing bib-overalls—not exactly typical trapper's clothing—though they were without traceable labels.

With respect to his personality, Johnson was a non-talker, generally antisocial, stubborn to a fault, cranky, impetuous; and, paradoxically, at times generous.

Albert Johnson's physical profile presents a man of average height, and though well-built, of average weight. He was five feet nine inches to five feet nine and one-half inches in height though he looked shorter because he was inclined to stoop.

Coroner J. A. Urquhart's description of the dead man showed that the body displayed no operation scars or evidence of fractures. Other than a mole in the centre of his lower back, there were no distinguishing marks.[4]

His age at death was estimated to have been between thirty-five and forty years.

Johnson's hair was described as light brown. In photos he seems to display a tuft of unruly hair on the back of his head as well as a cowlick that drooped over his right eye. His hair is parted on the left side. Johnson's beard was light brown.

One of the principal problems I was concerned about was the poor quality of the death photos for purposes of identifying Albert Johnson. First, some of his features were so gaunt from starvation while others were swollen from frostbite that he was virtually unrecognizable. Secondly, and even worse was the poor angle from which the photographer took the pictures, from underneath the chin, thus distorting the man's actual appearance. (This angle, in fact, is sometimes intentionally used to create a ghoulish effect in advertising or horror movies.)

In view of this, I prevailed upon a resident RCMP artist to portray Johnson as he would have looked without these facial

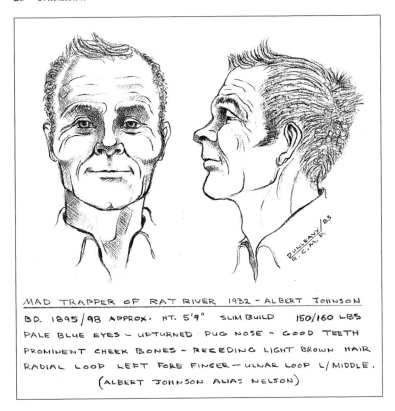

MAD TRAPPER OF RAT RIVER 1932 - ALBERT JOHNSON
BD. 1895/98 APPROX. HT. 5'9" SLIM BUILD 150/160 LBS
PALE BLUE EYES ~ UPTURNED PUG NOSE - GOOD TEETH
PROMINENT CHEEK BONES - RECEDING LIGHT BROWN HAIR
RADIAL LOOP LEFT FORE FINGER — ULNAR LOOP L/MIDDLE.
(ALBERT JOHNSON ALIAS NELSON)

Sketch of how the dead trapper might have looked when alive, based on death photos. RCMP ARCHIVES

distortions when he was alive. Corporal Patrick Dunleavy complied, providing me with portraits to match both the front and side views of the photographs. An Identikit portrait was also put together for me by the Alaska State Troopers.

The foregoing, then, was practically all that was available from the police, and from residents of Fort McPherson who had seen Johnson during the last eight or nine months of his life.

Fortunately, I got my first major clues when I met Ed Asp and

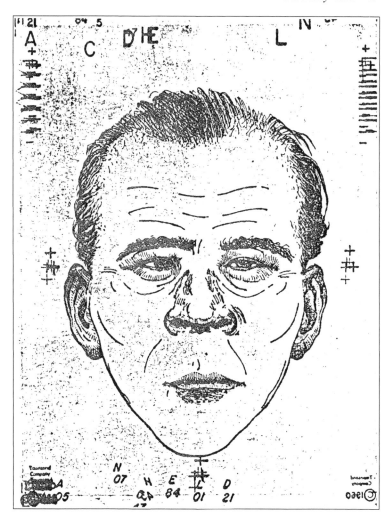

Identikit portrait generated from death photos. ALASKA STATE TROOPERS

other residents of Dease Lake, British Columbia, who told me they had known Albert Johnson when he trapped and worked in that area under the name Arthur Nelson in the mid 1920s. His residence there was established in 1937 when some trappers saw a death photo of Johnson in an article written by Harry F. Mullet in a detective magazine.[5]

When I first heard this evidence I was skeptical because Dease Lake seemed so far removed from the Arctic locale where Johnson was killed. However, this skepticism dissolved when I read an article in the *R.C.M.P. Quarterly*[6] in which Roy Buttle, the manager of the Taylor and Drury outfitters store at Ross River, Yukon Territory, was reported to have met Nelson at the post in 1927. Three important points arose out of his account.

First, Nelson had told trader Buttle he was "raised on a farm in North Dakota". Secondly, Nelson had informed Buttle that he had trapped the winter before in the area between Dease Lake and Teslin Lake. Judging by his purchases and other behaviour, this seemed to be incontrovertible. This eye-witness testimony from traders (who generally had to be shrewd observers of their customers) supported Dease Lake residents' claim that they had known Johnson under the Nelson name, and indicated that he may have been telling the truth about having come from North Dakota. If he were truthful at that time on the one point, there was reason to believe he was being truthful about the other. Thirdly, Buttle's description of the man he knew as Arthur Nelson meshed perfectly with Constable Millen's particulars on Albert Johnson. Buttle's account ran as follows:

"He was of average height, his well-proportioned frame packed about 170 pounds. His speech carried the trace of a Scandinavian accent and he seemed to walk with a habitual stoop. . . . He appeared to be in his early thirties."

In Arthur Nelson I had found a man to match the profile of Albert Johnson. I was suddenly hopeful that I could quickly establish his roots.

As in any such investigation, it makes sense to start with the obvious clues. I decided to take a direct approach in tracing Johnson, and wrote immediately to North Dakota in one fast attempt to identify him. It was logical to assume that the trapper may have been a First World War veteran. Since Johnson was estimated to have been between thirty-five and forty years old when he was killed in 1932, he would have been just the right age—between twenty-one and twenty-six years—for service in that war. The men of the posse chasing Johnson noted that he dug slit trenches for latrines, a characteristic common with those outdoorsmen who had once served in the army. This and the fact he was handy with guns could point in that direction.

I wrote to the Office of the Adjutant General of North Dakota and asked them if they had a roster of military personnel from that state who had served in the First World War. In the ensuing correspondence I discovered they not only possessed such a list but also a short biography of each man.

Acting on a hunch the trapper may at first have used his real name in the Yukon Territory, I requested the Adjutant General's Office to send me a list of all the "Arthur Nelsons" on file. There were seven. I tracked down each one, discarding each candidate as an insurmountable discrepancy came to light, until just one remained. This man was born in Illinois, and served with the 164th Regiment in the First World War. I learned there was an association of that regiment's veterans who published a newsletter, and they generously published a query I made concerning him. Three veterans answered my letters, one being John Spare, who had known Arthur Nelson as a youngster in Hunter, North Dakota. I sent Spare the death photos and asked him if this could be the same person he had met. He answered that it was. I wrote to the other two army chaps and they were in agreement that the photos "could be" the same Nelson they had known in the army.

I thought I had hit the jackpot right away. I congratulated myself on having unveiled one of the Arctic's great mysteries. Then this lead blew away like a thatched hut in a hurricane. The veteran Arthur Nelson's wife, whom I had managed to locate in Des Moines, Iowa, wrote to me to say that, on the contrary, her husband did not die in a far-off land, but had lived a long and happy life with her, and passed away in 1957. So the first hot lead went nowhere.

However, since I was on the North Dakota–First World War theme, I decided to try another tack, with the name "Albert Johnson". Back again I went to the Adjutant General's Office by letter, obtaining a list of all the Albert Johnsons who served. None of them fit either. It takes only a few lines to record it here, but tracing all the Albert Johnsons (there were six) and the Arthur Nelsons took me over a year and dozens of letters. I suppose it served me right for cutting corners. Sometimes a shortcut proves to be the longest way around.

The North Dakota lead still seemed viable, so I tried out another idea. I wrote to North Dakota's Department of Vital Statistics, seeking birth records of all the Albert Johnsons and Arthur Nelsons born there between the years 1892 and 1897. The one weakness in this tactic was the fact that the Mad Trapper may have emigrated from Europe with his parents to North Dakota and not been born there. On top of that, of course, I realized he also might *not* have lived in North Dakota—that is, he might have lied about it. The correspondence ended when the Department of Vital Statistics answered that birth records were classified material and such information could not be released to anyone other than to close relatives—or police, I suppose. I couldn't claim Albert/Arthur as a relative, so that saved me at least another year's work.

I was not unaware of another stumbling block in my research. If he used two different names in the north country, how many had he used prior to that? His real name could have been one of the many variations of Scandinavian names commonly adopted for use in the United states—Johnson, Jansen, Johnston, Johansson, Jonson; or Nelson, Nelsen, Nilsen, Nilson, Nielsen, Niewlson, etc. etc.

I finally threw up my hands on the quick route and junked the North Dakota effort completely. I was no Sherlock Holmes, nor even a good Dr. Watson. I concluded my manuscript for the first book and as an afterthought, mailed a copy to the North

Dakota State Historical Society, asking them to forward to me any leads that might cross their desk in the ensuing years.

Dismissing that effort from my mind, I decided to follow the more conventional and meticulous method of tracing Albert Johnson, and that meant running down every single lead, dispelling every wisp of a rumour. By sheer process of elimination I might one day discover who Albert Johnson really was.

CHAPTER 2

HE WALKED WITH A STOOP

A S THE NORTH DAKOTA LEAD began to peter out, I began the search that I fully expected now might take many years. But I was assisted near the outset by an incredible coincidence: I discovered a photo taken of Johnson when he was travelling in the Yukon as Arthur Nelson. The odds against finding such a snapshot were about as good as catching a rainbow. Or maybe some of my hunches *were* right.

The discovery came about during my search for "period" photos of areas through which Johnson was supposed to have travelled on his way north. "Period" pictures are simply pictures that are taken about the same time as the subject being written about; they give the reader a better visual idea of an era than any written word can do. One day I casually mentioned my search to a friend, Joe Lindsay, whose wife, Virginia, was the daughter of a former Yukon riverboat pilot by the name of Frank Slim. Lindsay told me Slim had faithfully carried a box camera with him in the twenties and thirties and had taken snapshots of just about every river town in the Yukon Territory.

I went to the senior citizens' home in Whitehorse and asked the old pilot if he had taken any photos of Ross River, the place where Roy Buttle had met Nelson in the summer of 1927. Frank said that he had, and obtained four which his son-in-law Joe possessed, and loaned them to me. They were amazingly clear and concise considering that they were taken with a plain old Brownie box camera forty years earlier. I looked them over, and in one spotted a blond man whom I thought could be a younger version of an old prospector and trapper I knew by the name of Fritz Guder. The man had the same shape of head and physical shape and unruly hair of Fritz. I noted the fact on the back of the snap. The Taylor and Drury supply warehouse was in the background, and since Nelson (a.k.a. Johnson) was supposed to have purchased the same make of rifle there as was found on Johnson when he was killed, the photo would be a good period piece for my book. I filed it away for future use.

Months later, I had the picture with me when I met Guder. The identity of the Mad Trapper had become a minor obsession with me in those years in preparation for the publication of my first "unfinished" book. I hauled out the photograph and asked Fritz if he would like me to make a copy of it for him. Fritz scanned the likeness, then looked at me quizzically—his eyes were still as keen as an eagle—and said:

"I don't know why you would want to give me a copy. That man isn't me. I had dark hair in my younger days, and I wouldn't have been in Ross River because I was never there when Frank piloted a boat up that way."

Fritz Guder had come to the Yukon in 1916, a raw immigrant from Germany. Hatred stirred up by war was at its apogee when he arrived. Former Mountie Poole Field spotted the *cheechako* in the community of Carmacks and, figuring the lad might be the target of some persecution, recommended that he go to the more remote village at Ross River to live. There he would be safe from anyone who might think him a German spy, and also far away from the tentacles of government.

Guder was quick to learn the rudiments of trapping, hunting, prospecting, and survival in the bush. He became so intrepid at what he was doing, he was probably the first and only person who ever killed a bull moose with a knife on dry land. He managed to do this with the help of fifteen pack dogs who kept the moose at bay while he fashioned a spear by binding a Wilson's butcher knife to a ten-foot pole. At the first jab the moose knocked Fritz down and kicked him, flattening a can of snoose he had in his back pocket. Fortunately, before the moose could finish him off, the pack dogs distracted the animal, and

Guder was able to scamper to safety. He continued the fight from the top of a bank against which the dogs had forced the moose. Finally the animal fell, weak from the loss of blood. Fritz finished him off with an axe. When I met Guder he still had the crushed tobacco can.

A short while after my talk with Guder and further study of the photographs it struck me that the blond-haired man in the snapshot I was toting around might actually *be that of the man Buttle knew as Arthur Nelson*, and that I knew as Albert Johnson. I returned to my twelve- by-twelve-foot cabin on Lambert Street in Whitehorse, and studied the picture under a magnifying glass. The most noticeable characteristic of the blond man was his "stooped" shoulders. This was one of the several factors in Johnson's appearance which figured in virtually every descrip-tion of him. I looked into my files on Johnson. After an hour and a half of frantic digging through the motley pile of letters, magazines, books, and other flotsam of a journalist, historian, and collector of memorabilia, I came up with a copy of the fall edition of the 1960 *RCMP Quarterly*. I reread the article, and the part about Nelson walking with a "habitual stoop" seemed to leap right at me from the page.

I restudied the snapshot. Nelson as described by Buttle cer-tainly could be this man. I compared death photos obtained from the Mounties with Slim's. There were some similarities, but I would have to get the picture enlarged. When I did this it was still inconclusive. The facial features disintegrated in the photo's grain even more when it was blown up. Unfortunately, the negative had been lost. The main stumbling block in my consideration of the photo as proof was the fact that it had been taken from too long a range. The death photos, on the other hand, were close-ups of Johnson's face; but they showed the man to be virtually a skeleton after almost two months of subsistence on the trail. Even if I were able to project a clear image of Nelson's countenance in the enlargement, it probably would not have been very similar to the death shots. Only one point stood out undeniably—and that was the stooped shoulders.

Arthur Nelson (left) with John Martin, Indian preacher and veteran guide of the famed Dawson City–Fort McPherson police patrols from 1904–1921. Photo taken by river-boat pilot Frank Slim at Ross River, Yukon, 1930.

I'm an eternal optimist. I suppose if I were not I would never have commenced this project in the first place, but I became slightly discouraged after staring at the Ross River photo for several hours. Finally I laid it aside. What was not there was not there. I could not wish the face into place.

I took the snapshot back to Frank Slim and asked him who the man was. Slim told me he knew him as Pete but could not recall his last name.[1] Slim said "Pete" had come to Ross River on the boat with him, having embarked at Fort Selkirk, a small settlement near the mouth of the Pelly River.

I asked him if he had ever seen the man before.

"Yes," Slim replied, "in 1927 I was staking some claims about sixteen miles south of Ross River and he came through camp on his way north from Teslin Lake."

I asked Slim if he had taken the picture after or before 1927. If it was before, the blond man could not have been Nelson because, according to Buttle, he did not arrive in the Yukon until that year.

"After," Frank said. "It was taken from the deck of the *Yukon Rose*, which replaced the *Thistle* which sank in 1928."

So now I had the name "Pete" to go on, and nearly discarded the photo in frustration—there were at least half a dozen "Petes" who had either lived in or used Ross River as a base for prospecting and trapping in the late twenties and early thirties. My ongoing research turned up a Pete Darling, a Picard, Boxen, Frederickson, Linder, and "Homebrew" Pete. I never did learn the last name of the latter, though he obviously had been a man of some character. I had no alternative other than to track down either each of the above named men, or at least someone who had known them closely.

The Ross River picture now became as important a fixture to my personal belongings as my wallet. I had it enlarged into an 8″x10″ with plenty of duplicates if I had to leave one somewhere. I noted that my friends began to look at me in a patronizing sort of way. Any mention of the name Albert Johnson would initiate a monologue which wouldn't end until they were asleep or walked away.

I drove to Dawson City looking for Jack Meloy, who had lived along the Yukon River since 1910 and knew just about everyone using the waterway.

Driving north from Whitehorse is not like driving around the block. Dawson City at that time was a distance of 355 miles over dirt roads that normally were in pretty fair condition except after a rain. Then potholes sprouted as quickly as mushrooms to batter my wheels as I passed over them. It's a scenic drive, however, and the vast panorama of the interior Yukon took my mind off the potholes.

For a part of the way I followed the majestic Yukon River, and pulled off the road to enjoy a view of historic Five Fingers Rapids. Here a side chute of the huge river pours over a steep drop that roils the main channel so violently that the early riverboats required a winch cable to pull themselves through the rapids on their trip upriver. If they slipped the winch they would ricochet off the walls of one of the rapids' "fingers" like a jai alai ball and sink. The opening of the road, about 1953, took care of that problem. Trucks replaced the boats, giving the artery of the river back to the moose and the bear and the caribou.

Leaving Five Fingers, I gradually climbed away from the Yukon to cross a range of hills into the valley of the Pelly River, one of the Yukon's larger tributaries. The route of pilot Frank Slim's boat in the early days took him from Whitehorse down the Yukon to Fort Selkirk. There he would pick up passengers destined for the Ross River post, as only a small draught boat like the *Yukon Rose* could make the 150-mile journey up the shallower waters of the Pelly River.

After leaving the Pelly I ascended another range of hills to the headwaters of Crooked Creek and followed that stream down to the Stewart River. The bridge here is about 175 miles upriver from the junction of the Stewart with the Yukon. And so it went from one watershed to another until I reached the south fork of the Klondike and descended that spruce-ornamented valley for forty or fifty miles into Dawson City.

Jack Meloy was a lean woodsman of eighty years with eyes as keen as a hawk's and a mind as crisp and clear as that of a twenty-year-old. For much of his life Meloy had been a packer and gold miner. Since 1910 he had lived on the banks of the Yukon River and there were few people resident in the Yukon Territory whom Jack did not actually know or know of.

I went to Meloy's house and asked him if he knew the various "Petes" I have mentioned and he said that he had known all of them. I showed him Slim's photo and he said the blond man was not one of the "Petes" mentioned; in fact, he did not recognize the person at all.

"I can tell you who is standing next to him, though," Jack said. "The Indian is John Martin. Martin was a preacher there."

While Meloy and I were talking, Mrs. Meloy scanned the picture. She was a sharp-eyed woman who had lived along the river for almost as long as Jack. Once, during an emergency, she "persuaded" a reluctant riverboat pilot to pull ashore at her cabin by putting a bullet through his pilot house.

She looked up and said, "There are two girls sitting next to the building on John Martin's left. They could be his daughters."

I took another look and saw that Mrs. Meloy was right. My repeated studies had failed to disclose this fact as the girls were wearing caps and men's shirts and pants. I learned one thing from Mrs. Meloy's appraisal. If you are studying a picture for any reason, don't depend solely on yourself; give it to others to scan. They'll see things you have invariably missed.

"One more thing," Meloy said, pointing to a lad carrying a sack on his shoulder in the foreground. "The boy could be John Martin's son, Robert."

If nothing else, these points indicated the Meloys knew what they were talking about. If they said no one named "Pete" was in the enlargement I could be reasonably sure that the snap was not of a local boy well known to most of the river people.

There was another person in the area who I thought might be able to answer that question. He was Joe Henry, a nephew of the late John Martin. Joe, though in his seventies, was camped in a tent sixty-eight miles up the Dempster Highway from its intersection with the Dawson City–Whitehorse road. I hopped into my car and drove out the south fork of the Klondike and turned left to follow that stream's north fork. It is a gradual climb to the crest of the Ogilvie Mountains at Mile 49. The view was superb and I stopped briefly to stare at Tombstone Mountain, a jagged peak to the west that knifes into the sky like a grave marker. From this point the road descends gradually into the south fork of the Blackstone River. The country opens up into mountain tundra and is virtually treeless. I followed Blackstone for about twenty miles until I reached Joe's camp. His tent was up and Annie, his wife, was tanning caribou skins when I walked in from the road. Joe put some tea on, and we conversed in the fragrant odour of freshly cut spruce boughs that made up the floor of his tent.

Joe and Annie were of a generation of Indians that constituted the last truly nomadic peoples in North America. Born in 1899, Joe spent the first thirty years of his life wandering in the huge wilderness that encompasses the northern Yukon Territory. In winter he and his family were constantly on the move, hunting moose and caribou. When they made a large kill they would camp next to it and trap around it. When the food was gone they would go off hunting again elsewhere and repeat the process. In summer they fished the streams and often travelled on the rivers in huge boats made out of moose skin. He recalled the largest he ever rode in was made of sixteen skins and had held four large families!

Joe and Annie were married in the church in 1920 and for ten years afterwards continued their nomadic life, but in 1930 they moved to Dawson City as schooling was needed for their rapidly growing family. They retained their wilderness roots by setting up a tent in spring and fall on the Blackstone River.

I showed Henry the photo and he confirmed that the Indian was John Martin, his uncle. Like the Meloys, Joe and Annie did not recognize the man standing next to Martin. I asked them if they recalled when John Martin had gone to Ross River. To me, of course, this was an important point. If John Martin had arrived at Ross River after 1930, the blond man could not have been Nelson, since other evidence showed he had by then left for points further north.

Joe and Annie consulted each other in their native tongue, then told me John Martin went to Ross River right after he was ordained an Anglican minister in Aklavik in the late twenties or early thirties, but they were not sure of the exact year. "Van Bibber family know," said Henry. "Martin's wife deliver baby for Mrs. Van Bibber on way to Ross River by dog team that spring."

Talk about puzzles: this was becoming a riddle to end all riddles. I felt like a chicken following bread crumbs. Every time I was about to quit, another tempting morsel would appear to lead me on. I thanked Joe for the information; then drank more of his brew, which was liberally laced with Labrador tea leaves. This stuff is a mild narcotic and puts you to sleep. I found that out about ten miles up the road when I had to pull off to take a nap.

CHAPTER 3

IN THE WAKE OF AN ELUSIVE SCANDINAVIAN

L ATER THAT YEAR I made a trip to Mayo, where I talked with George Van Bibber about the baby who had been delivered by Mrs. Martin. That was pretty easy for George to figure out: it was his brother Ted, and it was the spring of 1930. This meant that John Martin *had* been in Ross River during the time that Nelson could have been there. The photo would have to have been taken in the summer of 1930. Before that Martin was not there, and afterwards, if Johnson and Nelson were the same, Nelson was not there.

The date was established. Hitherto, I had been somewhat reluctant to set off in all directions before dating the photograph; now I was free to do that, and I quickly got underway. First, a letter to Peter Risbie, a friend of mine who lived in Ross River. I enclosed a copy of the photo and asked Pete to show it to Arthur John, who as a lad of fifteen or sixteen had known Nelson at Ross in the late twenties. I had previously interviewed Arthur John about Nelson, whom the Mounties had traced to Ross River, and he had informed me that the name he had known him by was "Dick". Apparently this guy had more names than alphabet soup has letters. Risbie finally ran into Arthur John in a mining camp somewhere near the headwaters of the Macmillan and showed him the blow-up of Slim's snapshot. John said unequivocally that the blond man in the centre was the man he had known as "Dick", with either Johnson or Nelson for a last name, but he thought it was Johnson.

Arthur John's senses were well honed by living over half a

century in the Yukon bush. Born in the gold camp of Living-stone Creek, of an Indian mother and a white father who was later killed in the First World War, Arthur John was as depend-able a reference as one could get. He had not only seen Nelson, but knew him, and earlier, when I had showed him death photos of Albert Johnson, he had said that Johnson was the same man he had known in Ross River. He had insisted, however, that his first name was either "Dick" or "Mick" and he stuck to his guns. It wasn't until a decade later that I found out how right Arthur John was.

Being a poor man's version of Sherlock Holmes doesn't mean one has quick perceptions, or maybe it should be the other way around—being of slow perception makes a poor man. At any rate, it was only ten years later that one day it hit me that possibly, somewhere along the river, the man Arthur John had known as Johnson had boarded one of the steamboats, and that his name had been recorded, as was the custom then, in the Dawson City newspaper. Privacy while travelling was unknown in those days. If a person went somewhere in the north, the newspapers printed the passenger lists. This even carried over into the airplane lists during my first years on the *Juneau Daily Empire* in 1963. (Eventually the practice came to an abrupt halt when the wife of one passenger wrote in wondering what she was doing on a flight with her husband when she had made no such flight with him. I never called him to find out, but since no murders ensued, either the wayward husband and his "wife" never returned to Juneau, or his real spouse clobbered him with a rolling pin when he stepped through the door.)

Having pinpointed the date of the photo to 1930, and having found out from Frank Slim that the blond man had boarded the boat at Fort Selkirk, I perused the Dawson City newspapers published in the summer of 1930. If Johnson had taken a steamboat upriver from Dawson City, his name might be on the list. Sure enough it was, and it backed up Arthur John's mem-ory. I quote from the *Dawson City News* of August 7, 1930: "Whitehorse Arrives and Departs—for Selkirk—John Ellis, *Dick Johnson*, Andrew, Billy Ena, E. Mellett, Frank Blanchard,

Sam Jonathan, and W. H. Atkinson" (italics added). The last named individual was Billy Atkinson, who also lived at Ross River. When Frank Slim took the photo of Nelson, he had also photographed his boat, the *Yukon Rose*, from the shore. Billy Atkinson is visible in that picture, lending credibility to the fact that Dick Johnson had indeed come up river on that trip and was the same man Arthur John knew under that name.[1]

In a short time I was back in Mayo again, this time to look up Lonnie Johnny, a native who trapped, hunted, and guided all over the Upper Stewart country and who had met Arthur Nelson several times at Lansing, a trading post on the upper Stewart. He lived with Norman Mervyn, whose father James Mervyn had operated the trading post at Lansing. RCMP Corporal Ed Zawrocha gave me directions to their place, a small cabin a few miles out of town. I knocked on their door one morning and after I explained my research, Lonnie and Norman invited me in for a coffee. I produced the Ross River photo and Lonnie took out his glasses to scan it. He nodded and verified that this was the man he had met at Lansing. Norman also recalled meeting the man at his father's store, though he had been a youth of only six or seven years at the time.

Back in Dawson City that same summer, I met Robert Martin, son of the preacher John Martin, in the Downtown Saloon. He had been a "special" constable for the Mounties in the thirties. Robert did not have his glasses with him and could not scrutinize the photograph for me, but he did tell me rumours had circulated around Ross River and Mayo that Albert Johnson had been involved in a murder in Idaho before he came north. Martin referred me to another former special constable, George Peter, who lived in Carmacks. George had served with the Mounties in the early thirties and made patrols between that town and Ross River. I was taken to Peter's house by Corporal Nick Veres. When I showed him the photograph, he said as far as he was concerned the man was Nelson.

George Peter confirmed another story that Arthur John had first told me, that an old Carmacks Indian named Scambella Jack had been far up Ross River with Joe and Jack Ladue, Paul

Sterriah, and Arthur John, in the late twenties, and met Nelson at his cabin at Sheldon Lake.

Later, Veres and I drove to the north side of Carmacks, past Roxie Carrière's trading post, and up to Jack's cabin. The old fellow answered the knock on his door and stepped out. The lines in his face were so deep they threw shadows in the morning sun. He looked warily at the Mountie, then at me, like a skittish wolf, but relaxed a bit when I brought out the blown-up photo and asked him if he recognized the man in it.

Scambella Jack scanned the enlargement for a minute, then said, "This taken long time ago."

I nodded.

Jack then added simply, "Seen him headwaters of Ross River. Many years ago. Not sure when."

This was another unassailable verification of the identity of the blond man. It left little doubt in my mind that this was indeed the man referred to as Arthur Nelson/Albert Johnson. This, then, was the only known photo taken of him alive.

I thanked Scambella Jack for his assistance and drove down to Roxie's trading post. Roxie is a friendly French Canadian from Manitoba. (His uncle had married Louis Riel's niece.) His great pride is his garden. He raises the tastiest vegetables this side of B.C.'s Okanagan. I told Roxie about visiting Scambella Jack, and he added that his own father had done some logging outside of Ross River in the late twenties, and knew Nelson. Unfortunately, Roxie's father died before I could interview him.

I realized that the supreme test of the photo lay in sending it to Fort McPherson, and here I almost met my Waterloo. I first mailed copies of the photo to John Robert in Fort McPherson. John Robert had tried to sell Johnson an outboard motor after the trapper had purchased a canoe from Abe Francis in Fort McPherson. He had also waited on Johnson and sold him supplies when he worked for Bill Douglas' trading post there. Robert wrote back and said, indeed, the snapshot was of Albert Johnson, the man he had met in 1931. Score another plus for me.

Now the bad news. I sent the photo to Abe Francis. Johnson had set up a little tent and lived across from Francis' camp for about two weeks in July of 1931, before setting out to build his cabin on the Rat River. Abe wrote back via a friend that he did not think the man in it was Albert Johnson. He contended that the morose Johnson would never be chatting with someone, as he appeared to be doing with John Martin.

The negative identification was a setback, but given the great preponderance of positive IDs, I let it go. Later I was to find out that Abe's eyes weren't too good, which tended to justify my dismissal of his verdict.

My research continued. I had met Peter Alexie's son, Robert, in Dawson City. Peter Alexie had participated in the Johnson manhunt and his son was acquainted with the local lore about the case. I sent Robert a copy of the photo. He showed it around to several old-timers who concurred that it was of Johnson, but none of them was specific about names.

I also mailed a copy to Constable Alfred King, then retired and living in Petrolia, Ontario. King had had only a fleeting glimpse of Johnson through the cabin window before he was shot; and again afterwards, when Johnson's body was brought into Aklavik. He said there was a strong resemblance but he was not sure. Photos were also mailed to Frank Riddell and Earl Hersey. Both Riddell and Hersey, officers in the Signal Corps of the Canadian Army, had taken part in the month-long chase, and had seen Johnson close up after he was killed. However, the Mad Trapper was so wasted away by that time that comparison was difficult. They saw strong similarities, but neither could say for certain that the Ross River photo was that of the dead man.

I continued to show the snapshot to other persons known to have met the trapper when he was in the Yukon. One was Ole Ostenstad, an octogenarian who lived in Keno, a mining camp near the headwaters of the McQuesten River. I drove there along a picturesque road that follows the valley of the Stewart River for part of the way. Steeped in local history, the head-

F. McPherson
n.w.T
Sept 29/70

Hi Dick,

Sorry for not writting any sooner.
Finding out about John Martin, he left
McPherson summer of 1929 for yukon,
he passed Dawson same season +
was in Ross River 1930, 31, 32 ——
So according to one old timer in
McPherson, the man in picture
beside John Martin is Albert Johnson.
And when Johnson passed Fort he
get his supples from N.C store when
they were still here; So this is
best I can do for you right now.
If you happen to come around
McPherson you'll find more about him

Write Back!

Best Regards
Robert Alexie
Ft McPherson n.W.T

```
                                  Ft. McPherson, N.W.T.
                          ·       Sept. 29/70


Hi Dick,

     Sorry for not writing any sooner.  Finding out about
John Martin, he left McPherson summer of 1929 for Yukon, he
passed Dawson same season and was in Ross River 1930, 31, 32.
So according to one old timer in McPherson, the man in
picture beside John Martin is Albert Johnson.  And when
Johnson passed Fort he get his supplies from N.C. Store
when they were still here, so this is best I can do for
you right now.  If you happen to come around McPherson
you'll find more about him.

Write Back!


                              Best Regards

                     (signed) Robert Alexie

                       Ft. McPherson, N.W.T.
```

Letter from Fort McPherson resident Robert Alexie identifies man in photo as Albert Johnson. Original written script is on preceding page. ROBERT ALEXIE

waters of the Stewart attracted prospectors like spruce bark attracts porcupines. The reason for this was the plethora of "lost gold mine" stories that have arisen in that country and for which Nelson, like others before him, may have been searching.[2]

I followed the Stewart as far as the river town of Mayo, which in earlier days was a port for shipment of silver ore from the mines at Keno and Elsa. The steamboats that plied the river and carried the ore were gone. Mayo's principal function now is as the headquarters for governmental services in the region. Mayo, Elsa, and Keno are virtually ignored by tourists, most visitors bypassing the communities to go to Dawson City, hub of the gold rush of 1898. In doing so, they miss one of the Yukon's finest side trips.

The highway leaves the Stewart River at Mayo and climbs over a low range of hills to the watershed of the south fork of the McQuesten River where the grade gradually ascends until the motorist is high above the valley. Here one can view the vast sprawl of the magnificent Potato Hills along the west bank of the McQuesten, and farther north the jagged peaks of the Wernecke Mountains, which rise up on the distant horizon like a crocus-tinged tidal wave. Mirroring the Werneckes are McQuesten and Hanson lakes, source bodies for the river, across which Johnson/Nelson tramped north in his search for solitude.

No one can drive up the Keno Road without being mesmerized by the tremendous expanse of coniferous forest that extends northward as far as the eye can see. Seemingly all of the mystery of the Arctic is contained in this scene, and Johnson himself, as a result of the tragedy of his last, lonely battle, emerges as a symbol of nature's stoic yet futile war against the incursions of civilization.

The panorama recedes from view as the road bears right and into the hamlet of Keno, which nestles against the foothills of the Werneckes like a delicate ptarmigan chick beside a grass hummock. It is an enchanting spot, and a place to which a visitor is inclined to return.

Ole Ostenstad came from Norway to the Yukon by way of the United States in 1910. It was a chilly spring morning when I drove to his cabin, and I wondered if he was home when I saw no smoke coming out of the cabin's stovepipe. You always worry about old-timers, especially during the cold days of winter when no smoke is seen spiralling out of a chimney; and you check right away to see if everything is okay.

Today everything was all right. The old Norwegian had just been sleeping a little late. He answered my knock and invited me in, and I immediately felt like I had just walked into the "stacks" of the newspaper section of the National Archives. You needed a floor plan to find the stove in Ole's place. If he had recycled the newspapers in his cabin he could have supplied the New York *Times* Sunday edition for a year.

Ole started a fire in the stove and in a short time the cabin was warm and comfortable. He put some coffee on to brew, and I went into my routine with the photo. Our only drawback was that Ole could not hear me. I shouted, but it was no use. I hoped the old boy's eyes were in better shape than his ears. Judging from the amount of newspapers and magazines strewn around the cabin I guessed they were. I wrote down the questions I had to ask him on the back of the envelope in which I carried the photo, and laid them in front of him.

Ole's eyes were fine. He had no trouble reading the questions, then his eyes moved to the Ross River enlargement, which he studied intensely. Without looking up he said, "That's Nelson all right. He spent about two weeks here. I remember him because I knew the man he stayed with. Nelson wasn't a talkative type, but I believe he was a Norwegian."

I asked Ole if he could recall the year. He was not sure. "He got into a fight with the police the next winter whatever year that was," Ostenstad said.

"He wasn't a Swede?" I asked.

Ole read my question and shook his head. "I don't think so, I believe he was a Norwegian," Ole said, sticking by his original recollection.

Ole was pretty helpful. We chatted about my unorthodox research methods for an hour or so before I took my leave. I could see though that the old man was pretty weak. The next step would be the old folks' home, a step that many of the old-timers fought bitterly because they figured going to a "home" was to put one foot in the grave.

When I took my leave, Ostenstad cordially invited me to stop by and offered to share the cabin any time I wanted. The old guy didn't have much but he was willing to share it. I would have liked to have taken him up on the offer but not long afterwards, as he had feared, the welfare people carted him off to the senior citizens' home in Whitehorse, as he had become too weak to feed himself and they couldn't let him die of starvation.

One thing about the hunt, it was taking me into every nook and cranny of the Yukon Territory. It turned out to be a great excuse to meet people, and in the course of my wanderings, gave me a rare opportunity to meet those Yukoners I would not normally encounter. Such occasions were not without their humour.

I knew that John Martin's brother, Richard, was still alive and living in the Sunset Home in Dawson City. Whoever applied the name "Sunset" to a senior citizens' home was not a brilliant public relations man. Ultimately, one resident of the home, or several, I cannot now recall, started squawking about it and did not let up until the name was changed. It is bad enough to have to take that step without having to be reminded that it might be your last.

The fact that John Martin and Nelson were standing close together in the Ross River photo indicated that they may have been carrying on a conversation—which might have included discussion of Nelson's ultimate destination in the northern Yukon Territory. Martin was from that area, having been born not too far from the scene of Albert Johnson's later death on the Eagle River. Before he became a preacher, John Martin had guided more police patrols over the 475-mile route between Dawson City and Fort McPherson than any other man. He knew every twist and turn of most of the trails in the northern Yukon, and was a walking library of information concerning the areas of the excellent trapping potential as well as some of the "lost mines" stories that invariably cropped up to lure prospectors northward. It would seem natural for a wanderer like Nelson to ask Martin about the vast northern interior. Even a recluse like the trapper could be expected to inquire about a region if going there gave him more of what he was looking for, that being freedom from association with other humans, yet with the possibility of profit.

I spoke with Richard about his brother. John had been two years younger, having been born in 1882. Richard had actually led the first Mountie patrol between Dawson City and Fort McPherson and had then turned it over to his brother, John. I was not unaware that Richard and John were tall men as far as northern Indians went, and while talking with him, surmised that if I took his height it might give me an approximate idea of John's. In turn, since John and Nelson were standing beside one another in the photo, this would help to establish Nelson's height. However, Richard, at ninety, said he had lost a few inches. I asked the old-timer if I could measure him and he said it was okay. I got a book and had Richard stand against the wall in the old folks' home, placed the book on his head and used it to draw a pencil mark on the wall. Richard, though he was completely blind, and had been since 1927, had never lost his sense of humour. He said something to the effect, "Hey, I'm not ready for the box yet!" A nurse and I heard the remark at the same time and we both smiled. Richard's height, allowing for the degenerative effects of age, was five feet nine inches. In the Ross River photo, the two men appear to be very nearly the same height, so this adds to the identification of the blond-haired man as Johnson since his measurements by Doctor Urquhart were five feet nine to nine and a half inches.

A weaker man than Richard probably could not have survived the mental anguish after losing his eyesight. When he was a youngster he had pulled a knife along a stick he was sharpening, and it slipped and put out his eye. Then in 1927, shortly before he was to be ordained as an Anglican minister, he was caribou hunting on the Blackstone River when he fired a rifle that blew up in his face and put out his remaining good eye. His son, Joe, though only a lad in his early teens, had raced a dog team eastwards seventy-five miles to get help from his cousin, Joe Henry. They returned, and in an epic race to Dawson City brought the wounded man in. But it was too late to save his eyesight. Bruised but not beaten, Richard went on to become ordained when he recovered and he was an effective minister at Moosehide on the Yukon River for many years. Obviously I did not have to show Richard the photograph.

Nonetheless, he did give me one additional strange clue regarding Johnson that he had heard from relatives of his who lived in the Alaska town of Eagle, located downriver from Dawson. The Malcolm family told him that Albert Johnson had passed through their area about 1930. They said several Indian trappers once met him camping in the bush. The trappers recalled Johnson not only for his quiet ways, but because he had claimed he was reading about himself in a newspaper. Later the same point was made to me by another Indian who had lived downriver. It was such an odd sort of comment that I wrote it down twice in my diary, and this led to my checking out the lead stories in Dawson newspapers published in the summer of 1930.

The *Dawson City News*, like every paper in North America, had splashed the unsolved murder of Chicago reporter Jake Lingle all over its front pages throughout the summer of 1930. Dawson City was on the telegraph line, so their coverage was up to the minute. Witnesses to the murder claimed that a blond man about five feet ten inches tall had shot Lingle and then gotten away. I thought of the odd clue of Richard's and the Chicago murder, and of the fact that Earl Hersey had opined that Johnson was a gangster from Chicago because he muttered not a word to anyone, fought to the death, and carried no identification—common denominators with "hard cases" who expired in gangland gun battles with the police. Suddenly, for a second it all seemed to fit together—the secretiveness and the cold calculation. For a time, I almost wanted to believe the exotic theory myself.

Mobsters could kill mobsters, but when a member of the press was gunned down, it was real news, though later it was found that Jake Lingle was not so Simon-pure as had once been supposed by his associates.

The lead paragraph in the *Dawson City News* on August 7 (the same edition as the one in which the names of Dick Johnson and Billy Atkinson appear on a list of passengers heading upriver to Fort Selkirk) under the title LINGLE SLAYER SUSPECT UNDER ARREST IN CHICAGO, reads as follows: "Chicago, July 21—Thomas Abbott, secretly sought as the actual slayer of Alfred 'Jake' Lingle, veteran Chicago *Tribune* reporter, was captured last Saturday after a spectacular chase, while hundreds lined the streets cheering." And in the last paragraph: "Abbott denied any part in the Lingle murder. . . ."

DAWSO[

DAWSON, YUKON TERRTIORY, CANADA, THURSDAY,

NEWSPAPERS NOW AFTER CHI GANGSTERS

CHICAGO, June 11. — (Special to The News.)—The newspapers of Chicago have accepted the challenge of gangland, which came with the cowardly assassination of Alfred "Jake" Lingle, a reporter for the Chicago Tribune. The Chicago Herald-Examiner, a Hearst morning newspaper, today offered a reward of $25,000 for the capture and conviction of Lingle's slayers, bringing the total rewards posted by Chicago newspapers to $55,000.

Police Ordered to Fight Gangsters

CHICAGGO, June 12.—(Special to

CHINESE VICTORI NAT

SHANGHAI, J The News.)—Thr ist government t torious Kwang; armies Wednesd; columns upon the The progress o and the continu Northern rebels Honan provinces the situation ex China's governme

Chief Japa

TOKIO, June News.)—Climaxin

The Dawson paper, like all newspapers across Canada and the U.S., splashed stories of the "gangland wars" across its front pages in the early 1930s. DAWSON NEWS

He was later released, and the search continued. If Johnson were the guilty party it would have been hard for him to have missed reading the story if he even glanced at the Yukon newspaper.

The Lingle theory was an interesting one. However, for Johnson to have been involved and to make a safe getaway, he would have needed extensive underworld connections. Furthermore, my own accumulating research suggested that he was nothing more than a trapper who became "bushed" from living too many years alone. The Chicago mobster theory was the most "glamorous" of all the rumours that circulated after Johnson's death, but it would take more evidence than I then had, I had to soberly admit, to make it appear credible.

CHAPTER 4

BILL JOHNSON AND THE BLACK LAKE MYSTERY

T O THIS POINT, I have discussed my attempts to establish Albert Johnson's identity through firsthand accounts of people who knew him as either Albert Johnson or Arthur Nelson. There are, however, other aspects of the case which, when patched together, gave additional clues as to Johnson's identity.

Judging by the shadows, the Ross River snapshot was probably taken around midday. (I neglected to ask pilot Frank Slim some of these details, and he too died before I could go back.) Three people in the picture, including Nelson, appear to be picking their teeth. Probably something tasty had been brought up on the boat and everyone had sampled it right away, or they had just finished lunch. Furthermore, Nelson was picking his teeth on the left side of his mouth. I recalled from Dr. Urquhart's description that the man killed by the Mounties had fewer teeth on his right side of his mouth than on his left, so he would have done most of his chewing on the left side of his mouth.

One swallow (no pun intended) doesn't make a summer, but a flock of them sure helps. The checklist of similarities between the notes in Johnson's death description and the man in Slim's photo included the following. The man at Ross River and the death portraits of Albert Johnson both showed hair that was unruly, with a cowlick as Dr. Urquhart remarked—though being chased for six or seven weeks at forty below zero doesn't bring out the best in a man's grooming. The Ross River picture also showed a man with a jaw and prominent cheek bones like those of Albert Johnson.

Frontal shots of Albert Johnson in death show that he had "sad eyes" or "heavy lids". The same trait seemed to be present in the Ross River picture. Nelson's fair hair matched the description of Albert Johnson's and the "stooped" shoulders stood out like a hump on a moose.

Through interpolation of the heights of Richard and John Martin I established that Arthur Nelson was five feet nine inches tall, or within the estimates of that of Albert Johnson.

In addition to the above, Ole Ostenstad, under close examination, had stuck to his belief that Nelson was a Norwegian.

Another obvious element in Nelson's character was his predisposition to using aliases. One wonders how he managed to keep track of who he was—Albert Johnson, Arthur Nelson, Dick Johnson, or Pete something or other?

Soon after Albert Johnson's death, rumours concerning his identity saturated Canada and the United States. These accounts placed the trapper in numerous roles. Many, though appearing baseless, proved the old adage that "where there is smoke there is fire." There were a number of leads that warranted further investigation and I decided to pursue them.

One of the most recent accounts (at the time I was conducting my investigation) that claimed to identify Johnson was published in the *Vancouver Sun* in the seventies. Why these accounts still surface, unbidden, is a mystery; perhaps the desire of oldsters to "tell what they know" one last time before it is too late, to maybe clean up something that has teased the back of their minds for years and years.

Whatever the reason, a Mr. and Mrs. A. C. Benson told reporters they were certain a man they knew in the twenties was the unidentified trapper. They had good evidence. A photograph furnished by them did bear some resemblance to the man killed by the Mounties. They said he was a blue-eyed Swede with sandy hair, about the same height and weight, good with an axe and saw, who lost his money to sharpers in a bad business deal in Vancouver. The latter was reason enough for him to be embittered with society. He had been a trapper in the Northwest Territories before going to Vancouver. And, like one rumour about Albert Johnson, his partner was a Frenchman.

The Bensons went into considerable detail about this man, though they did not recall his first name. Benson, who ran a shipyard, met Johnson when the latter asked Benson's opinion concerning the purchase of a fishing boat he and his partner planned to use along the British Columbia coast. Benson said the boat was too small and advised against their buying it. The two men took his advice. Instead, they bought into a fuel—wood and coal—business.

Benson and Johnson became friendly, and on a number of occasions the Bensons invited him over to have dinner with them. Often Mrs. Benson would serve Swedish meatballs which were a favourite of the former trapper. The Bensons found out that Johnson was from Karlskrona, Sweden. He and his partner had made a considerable amount of money trapping the year before and decided to go into business in Vancouver and start a new life. Johnson and his partner failed to prosper in the business and in a short time lost it. Ultimately, after failing to find a job, both men returned north to their trap line.

"He went back with a grudge," Benson said. "I never heard from him again."

It seemed that, at long last, Albert Johnson was identified. But it was not to be.

In the course of my research on Johnson, I had read Erik Munsterhjelm's autobiographical book *The Wind and the Caribou*.[1] On page 47, Munsterhjelm described a Swedish trapper he knew by the name of Bill (he did not give the last name) who, with his partner Joe, made a great deal of money one year trapping marten and white fox along the edge of the barren grounds at Snowbird Lake, northeast of Stony Rapids, Saskatchewan. The two men went to Vancouver and purchased a tugboat which they soon were forced to sell because business was poor.

Bill Johnson of Stony Rapids, Saskatchewan, was mistakenly identified as the "Mad Trapper", but may have committed one of the crimes often attributed in rumours to Albert Johnson. A. C. Benson is on the left. VANCOUVER SUN

While in Vancouver, Joe got tangled up with a widow and married her. The two men then bought into a poolroom and lost money on that. Summer came around and they had to sell again. The two trappers decided to go back to their permanent base at Stony Rapids. Joe gave the receipts from the sale of the poolroom to his bride. Later, he even lost money on that "investment" as his wife sued him for non-support and obtained a divorce. So ended the Vancouver adventure for the two men. Needless to say, neither ever went "outside" again.

Bill and Joe sounded so much like those met by the Bensons, that I sent Munsterhjelm a copy of the article and photo that had appeared in the *Vancouver Sun*. Sure enough, Munsterhjelm confirmed that the man in the photo was the same individual he had known at Stony Rapids, a man named Bill Johnson. Moreover, the writer told me, *this* Bill Johnson had drowned while duck hunting near that community in 1940, eight years after the death of Albert Johnson. Bill Johnson's partner Joe Marion was originally from Wyoming. Marion was part Cherokee, and probably of French descent. So, this lead was explained away.

By a strange coincidence, another story brought my research back to Stony Rapids. At first it seemed to have nothing to do with the Benson article. Later, an odd twist brought the Benson account back into focus.

The reason I had read *The Wind and the Caribou* in the first place was because of a lead I had received concerning Albert Johnson from Tom Coleman, an ex-Mountie who had run across the trapper's trail in the Yukon. Coleman told me he had heard a radio broadcast in 1934 concerning an incident that sounded to him like a murder Albert Johnson could have committed. In the early twenties, a trapper by the name of Peterson lived near a large creek branching off the northeast corner of a Black Lake. He died in his cabin sometime during the spring. No one seemed to know how or why. His furs, money, a gold watch, and a mahogany chest were missing. His skeleton was found fully clothed with a bottle of liquor amongst the remains.

In 1934, a prospector found Peterson's chest among the willows on the shore of Middle Lake. The chest was empty. Its finder, a man named Oscar Johnson, claimed there must have been foul play in the case because the chest was found empty fifty miles away from its owner's cabin.

Coleman could not recall where the event took place other than the names of the lakes. And to further complicate matters, when I went to the maps, I found there were scores of lakes in the country called "Black" or "Middle". The fact is, there are hundreds of small lakes in Canada's north still unnamed, or known locally by "unofficial" names, or with the same names. A year or two went by and I still had not found out where the story had taken place. One day I was visiting RCMP Corporal Ray Dyck and his wife at their home in Mayo, Yukon Territory, and we got to talking about some of Dyck's former postings. He told me he had been stationed at Stony Rapids, Saskatchewan. He recounted something about fishing or hunting at a place called Black Lake. Immediately I recalled the Peterson story and asked him if there was a Middle Lake near Black Lake. He said there was. I asked him about the incident involving Peterson and he remembered old-timers mentioning it but he did not know the details. He told me the incident was mentioned in Munsterhjelm's book. It spelled out the affair more accurately, but the story of Peterson's death was still quite vague.

Eventually I contacted Corporal M. R. Devaney, NCO in charge of the RCMP detachment at Stony. He wrote back and told me the son of the special constable who had investigated the death in the early twenties (with a Saskatchewan provincial policeman) was currently a special constable for the Mountie detachment. Devaney asked him about the case and found out that Peterson had suffered an unusual death because of his great strength.

Peterson had been carrying a huge log and slipped and fell backwards, the log crushing his chest. The solitary trapper staggered back to his cabin and fell into his bunk. He wrote a note telling of his difficulty, and placed a pan next to his bed into which he vomited blood. To ease his pain he opened a bottle of liquor and drained it, before dying miserably.

Months later, when Saskatchewan provincial police finally checked out the cabin on their periodic circuits, they found Peterson's skeleton, the empty bottle of liquor, and the pan with the dried blood, and noted that his steamer trunk was missing.

What had happened to the trunk? It would appear that the trunk was removed after Peterson's death and was not the cause of it. Someone had obviously taken the trapper's valuables, emptied the trunk, and dumped it along the shores of Middle Lake. Most likely the trunk was carried away on a dog sled in the spring. If it had been summer it could easily have been disposed of in the lake.

In looking around for potential culprits in the Peterson affair the logical place to start was in the area of the offence. Did anyone in the area suddenly exhibit riches that they had not done beforehand? Apparently not. However, from a vantage point of fifty years' distance, perhaps a better perspective is possible.

The first clue in the case was that of the Bensons' meeting with Bill Johnson and Joe Marion in Vancouver. They said the year they met the two partners was 1927. It is not known how long the two were there before meeting the Bensons, but it could have been anywhere from one to five years.

The second and third leads were provided by Munsterhjelm's observation that Bill and Joe had had a great year trapping at Snowbird Lake. He estimated their trapping earned them six to seven thousand dollars the winter before they went to Vancouver. This by itself is not incriminating. It was possible for two men to have made that much. However, the question of the location of Snowbird Lake in relation to Peterson's cabin may be significant.

Out of curiosity I went to the map and found Snowbird Lake. Its location gave a strong hint of culpability. If you were going to go from the lake to Stony Rapids after a winter's trapping, your route would pass in close by Peterson's cabin. Later, to doublecheck, I asked Lorne Terry and Jack McNevin, two men who prospected that area, if the trail went where I supposed. They confirmed that it did.

It is easy to visualize passersby like Marion and Johnson (or others who may have travelled by Peterson's hut) taking the trunk. I described the case to an old prospector I know, and asked him what he would have done if he had come to Peterson's cabin after a winter's trapping and found the trapper dead. The old fellow thought about it for a while and said, "I would collect his gear and take it to the authorities."

I complimented him on his honesty.

"But," he added, "if there was a heavy trunk, with money, and furs and valuables, and I knew Peterson had no next of kin, I might get awfully tired of lugging that trunk on the sled in the soft snows of spring and toss it away. And when I tossed that away, I would say to myself, 'I can use the furs, money, and watch a lot more than any policeman.' I would just keep the furs and the money and the watch and forget about it. What the police didn't know wouldn't hurt them, and it certainly couldn't hurt Peterson."

This, of course, is only a reasonable guess as to what took place. I'll let the reader be the final judge. Coleman, like most ordinary people, of course, heard about a murder here or there, but was not privy to final results of the police investigation. Thus the rumours of "unsolved" crimes continued to circulate for years, giving life to the fantasies about Johnson as a pathological madman and killer.

In finding out the cause of Peterson's death I not only exonerated Albert Johnson as a suspect, but also washed out another lead concerning the Mad Trapper. This originated as a result of my correspondence with Olive Frederickson, author of the book *The Silence of the North*.[2]

In her book, Mrs. Frederickson mentioned two trappers she and her husband met at Fort Smith, N.W.T., in 1922. They were Nels Nelson and Pete Peterson (a.k.a Anderson). Both men had worked on the railroad to Fort McMurray, Alberta. Her reference intrigued me, so I wrote to her and asked if she thought either one of the two men could have been Albert Johnson.

She wrote back and said that Pete Peterson, at least from a personality standpoint, would match up with Albert Johnson. She dismissed the possibility of Nels Nelson being Johnson because Nelson had been an outgoing man who smoked and drank and generally had a good time. Peterson was the exact opposite. He was a quiet man with ice-blue eyes, steel hard, that looked right through a person. He weighed 185 pounds, and it was all muscle. She said she often saw Peterson at his tent camp, which was about seventy-five feet from her cabin. He would sometimes stand or sit in one spot or lean against a tree and just look at the sky for an hour or more. She wondered why he was inclined to look so sad at times, and asked Nels Nelson about him. Other than saying he was hardworking and generous, Nels gave her no clue to Peterson's past. Mrs. Frederickson recalled that she never saw Peterson smile, and though he was not a hostile person, she wondered if he might have been a little "bushed". The last she saw of the two men, they were loading a wagon to take over the portage to Fort Smith. Peterson's tremendous strength was evident from the ease with which he could load three one-hundred-pound bags of flour to each one wrestled up by Nelson.

Munsterhjelm's reference to an incident that demonstrated the strength of a man named Peterson tended to confirm that the Peterson at Stony Rapids and Black Lake was the same man Mrs. Frederickson knew. Erik had heard stories of the man's tremendous strength when he arrived at Stony Rapids in 1934. Since Munsterhjelm was six feet six inches and weighed around 250 pounds, local residents challenged him to carry a boulder which Peterson had toted one hundred feet on a bet. Munsterhjelm told me he could not even budge it. He said a number of men had moved to Stony Rapids from the Fort McMurray area in the early twenties. Among them were Oscar Johnson, Alex McCaskill, Joe Marion, Bill Johnson, Fred Erickson, and probably Peterson.

By establishing Peterson's death, I destroyed another rumour that had appeared to tie in with Albert Johnson in the Yukon Territory. Ole Christianson, who for years owned the Occidental Bar in Dawson City, thought that he had known Albert Johnson in Fort McMurray. But from his descriptions it is reasonable to believe that he, like many others, mistook either Bill Johnson or Pete Peterson for Albert Johnson.

It is amazing how a blanket can be woven from only a few threads.

CHAPTER 5

THE EX-COP HYPOTHESIS AND ANOTHER COLD TRAIL

T HE MOST PREVALENT of all rumours about Albert Johnson was the one that hinted that he had been a former Mountie and/or a provincial policeman. A certain war veteran, Harry Johnson, was both. While looking for material on the Mad Trapper in a Wrangell, Alaska, newspaper, I came across the news about Harry.

Harry Johnson enlisted in the First Remount Depot, C.A.V.C. at Valcartier, Quebec, on September 22, 1914. Later he was transferred to the 13th Infantry Battalion and served in Canada, England, France, and Belgium. Harry was shot through the arm in the great Allied offensive on the Somme in September, 1918, afterwards being returned to Canada and honourably discharged at Regina, Saskatchewan, for "physical unfitness".

After discharge he joined the Royal Northwest Mounted Police at Regina.[1] He was twenty-two at the time. To the credit of the Force, he did not last long with them. He was discharged as "unsuitable" in July, 1919.

Subsequently, Johnson enlisted in the Saskatchewan Provincial Police and served half a year. He then resigned to marry a girl named Katie Craft[2] and went to live with her at her father's farm near Jasmin, Saskatchewan, which is located about forty miles west of Yorkton. Here, he became involved in an argument with his father-in-law, Jacob, and, being an opportunist, Johnson formally charged him with an incestuous relationship with his daughter (Johnson's wife). Harry apparently schemed to obtain the farm this way. Craft took umbrage at his son-in-law's charge, and with his sons, threatened Johnson with a pitchfork. In the resultant mêlée, the war vet killed his wife's brother, Peter, by shooting him with a 12-gauge shotgun. Johnson claimed self-defence in court, and was acquitted by a jury that was out for only an hour and a half.

It was not long before Harry Johnson was immersed in trouble again. He emigrated to the United States and went to work for a salmon cannery near Juneau, Alaska. Soon afterwards, he was discharged from his new job on suspicion of theft. Then he moved to Juneau where he worked for a restaurant, but he lost that job for mishandling funds.

At this point, Johnson resumed a boxing career that he had once pursued in Canada. He fought three fights at Elks' Smokers, winning two and drawing a third. Some of those who saw him box said he was a better than average pugilist. He claimed to have won the Canadian welterweight title in a bout in Calgary. Rumours that Albert Johnson may have been an ex-pug probably originated here.

On September 24, 1923, the bodies of two prostitutes, Hilda Weiss, and Luella Boadway (a.k.a. Billie Mason) were found at their "resort" on Lower Front Street in Juneau. The Boadway woman had been shot once in the head and once through the hand. Juneau police guessed that the same shot inflicted both wounds: as if the Boadway girl had instinctively held up her hand to ward off the bullet. The Weiss woman was shot four times. She had also been badly beaten, her skull having been fractured and her face battered. Marks of hands on her throat indicated she had been choked. The rooms in which the women were lying were spattered with blood. There were also stains on the walls of a stairway leading to the upper floor. Obviously, one of the girls had attempted to escape in that direction.

Less than four hours after the crime, Harry Johnson was arrested in the Bergman Hotel. A search of his room dis-

Harry Johnson, probable subject of the ex-cop hypothesis. The irascible Johnson murdered at least three people, but was deported in 1934, and was not the Mad Trapper. US DEPT. OF JUSTICE

closed that he had just finished washing a suit of clothes as well as his shoes, both of which were later found to be stained with blood.

Since the evidence was largely circumstantial, and plea-bargaining was not unknown even then, Johnson got off with a life sentence after pleading guilty to second-degree murder.

It should be pointed out that on two occasions in testimony in the previous Craft murder case, members of the family had attested that Harry Johnson went into homicidal "fits". On one occasion he had tried to kill one of Craft's sons with an iron poker which was wrestled away from him. Another time he threatened the family with an axe. They believed he was not wholly responsible for his actions, having been "shell-shocked" during the war.

Johnson was sent to McNeil Island Prison in Washington state in December 1923, and then to Fort Leavenworth, Kansas.

I thought that if by chance he had been discharged from prison in the late twenties, he could have been Albert Johnson. However, further research indicated that Harry Johnson was in Fort Leavenworth at the same time of Albert Johnson's shootout with the Mounties, and was transferred to Alcatraz when it was newly opened for incorrigible federal prisoners on September 4, 1934. A little over a year later he was released and deported to England, his home country. It makes one wonder what sort of mischief he got into after that.

One can readily see why many people in Saskatchewan later thought they had known Albert Johnson, though the man they actually recalled was Harry Johnson. Harry was the same height with brown hair, light complexion, and weighed 150 pounds—not unlike the description of Albert. His crankiness and hot temper matched the explosive actions of the unidentified trapper. Harry had been a policeman and then disappeared from the prairies after the murder trial. Not knowing he was in jail, people reading about the Yukon's Albert Johnson would have thought he was the Johnson from Saskatchewan.

Former Special Constable Robert Martin's tip about Albert Johnson having been from Idaho was another familiar one. An article by W. R. ("Wop") May recalling his experiences as the pilot the Mounties hired in the Johnson manhunt appeared in *True Detective Mysteries Magazine* in the fall of 1932, and proposed this idea.[3]

May noted the mystery surrounding Albert Johnson's identity, and claimed he saw a strong resemblance between the trapper and a photo of a man named Coyote Bill, who was wanted for murder in the state of Idaho. May's source was a story by Detective Luke May (no relation) which had appeared in an earlier issue of the magazine the same year.

Wop May neglected to give Coyote Bill's last name or the year in which the offence was supposed to have been committed. One would think that if there had been something to the pilot's surmise, it would have surfaced after forty years. However, big trees can out of little acorns grow, so I decided to look into the case.

I obtained a copy of Luke May's article. May was one of the foremost sleuths in the West at that time. Coyote Bill, whose last name was Banty, was wanted for the murder of Wilbur Breckinridge, foreman of the Irrigation District of New Sweden near Idaho Falls, on the night of March 24, 1916. There was a picture of Coyote Bill with the story.

I compared it with the death photos of Albert Johnson and noted that there were similarities. Like Johnson, Banty showed a receding hairline, bulbous nose, ears low set and close to the head, thin lips, and an overall cranial likeness. Coyote Bill's physique was also similar in another feature of Johnson described by Wop May: he had no chest hair. The snapshot of Banty showed him with his shirt off in an old-style boxer's pose with the right arm extended and the left arm crooked against his side. That Coyote Bill had been a prize fighter tended to reinforce a statement to me by an RCMP identification expert that the death photos of Johnson showed a fold in his left ear. This was particularly common to men with experience in the ring.

The similarities were offset by several differences: Banty's dark hair and eyes (though photos of blond individuals in black and white photos can sometimes be misleading) and his age. Banty would have committed his alleged offence in 1916. He looked about thirty in his photo which meant he would have been around forty-five in 1932, a shade older than the age estimated for Johnson. Nowhere did the detective mention Banty's height, weight, or hair or eye colour.

ng a Slayer in the Craters of the Moon

o old that it would uccessful at all, to l prepared a letter um we had found, olice and sheriff's that source all I

Evans' state- l me. First ndered if he n that bunk- d skull And two bandits

"Coyote Bill." First a suspect and then appar- ently exonerated, only to become a suspect again in this strange case

bandits waited so long in house? The burglary c been completed in half Were they waiting for Will inridge? In other words Evans' attempt to im direct suspicion a Bill, a clever ide attention from else? Or, bandits wait bunkhouse train time? The Ida Police assur the roomin search wa thorough been made train pull The two off were at the station ; knew Coyote Bill; b sure he had not boa train. Several men ha on the train; but no the description of the or Coyote Bill. So, despite Dan Ev tial identification, I w. to admit that Coyote pretty thoroughly el from the picture. Coyote Bill did not night train he was Idaho Falls; and in tha could most certainly find him. My attention was now turned to

Coyote Bill Banty of Idaho, another small-time bandit from the U.S. who ended up in Canada, but probably died in a mine cave-in in the Cassiars in northern British Columbia. TRUE DETECTIVE MYSTERIES MAGAZINE

The superintendent of the New Sweden Irrigation District at the time of the incident was Joe Gull. He carried large amounts of cash on his person because in his position as superintendent he often bought and sold hay and paid his employees in cash.

Coyote Bill trapped beavers and muskrats in the company's canals. The animals were considered pests for which the Irrigation District paid a bounty and Banty collected his money from Joe Gull. So he would have been familiar with Gull's work habits and with the large sums of cash the superintendent carried with him.

On the night of the murder, two men wearing bandanas over their faces, hats, and heavy coats to conceal their clothing entered the bunkhouse of the company. They pulled out handguns and told the bunkhouse's four occupants it was a stick-up. One of the occupants, Dan Evans, thinking the whole thing was a joke, kicked out at the burlier of the two bandits and was immediately shot, the slug grazing his skull. The same man then thumped Evans over the head so hard with the barrel of his gun that it broke the barrel. However, Dan remained conscious in spite of the two wounds. He and the other three men were tied up and then relieved of their watches, money, and valuables. As the two robbers turned to leave, Evans unthinkingly told them not to bother the foreman who was not home but would be returning from a club meeting in Idaho Falls. This innocent comment may have led to Breckinridge's death, for the thieves waited to waylay the foreman, possibly thinking Evans meant Gull. Sure enough, the unsuspecting Breckinridge walked right into the two desperados a few minutes later. The men in the bunkhouse heard three shots ring out and then there was silence. Finally one of them escaped his bonds only to find Breckinridge dead with three bullet holes in him. His wallet was completely empty, strongly suggesting the theft was the motive for the murder.

The population of Idaho rose up in arms over this senseless shooting and immediately raised money to hire detectives to track down the killers. Luke May's agency was called and May undertook what he at first thought would be a simple case. He expected that local thugs had done the job.

He soon found out otherwise. Before his investigation was

completed, he had questioned scores of people and had chased Coyote Bill through half of Idaho, including the wild, arid wastes of a forbidding area known as "Craters of the Moon".

Once I knew the date of the robbery it was relatively easy to check the local newspapers in Rexburg and Idaho Falls to find a description of the killers. One of the murderers was a large man and the other small. One was estimated to be about five feet nine or ten inches, with broad shoulders and weighing from 180 to 190 pounds. He showed some cleverness with a gun by spinning one on his finger. The other man was five feet seven and weighed about 140 pounds. The latter proved to be Alfred Metzner, whose photo appeared in the Luke May story. He quite obviously was too short and slight to have been Albert Johnson.

Luke May eventually tracked down Metzner, who pleaded guilty to second-degree murder and was sentenced to "from ten to twenty years" in the state penitentiary.[4] The judge let Metzner off lightly because of his youth and the fact that the older man, Bill Banty, was the moving force behind the grisly crime.

The youth described several of Banty's habits. One was to sleep twenty to thirty yards away from his campfire, and therefore be the first to awaken if anyone approached. Another was to travel only at night when he was on the run. Metzner was of the opinion that Coyote Bill had drifted north into the Canadian wilds.

May continued to search for Coyote Bill but to no avail. Persistent reports arose later that Bill had married an Indian girl and was living near Great Slave Slake in the subarctic. Since Luke May's story was written sixteen years after the murder occurred, it seemed to tie in well with Albert Johnson because the trapper had had five freshwater pearls in his pocket when he was killed.[5] These are fairly common in Great Slave Lake. Could it be possible that Banty was Albert Johnson?

I wrote to many people in Idaho before eventually contacting Milo Beckman, who had managed the New Sweden Irrigation Company for twenty-six years and had lived in the community all of his life. Beckman wrote that his wife, Emma, (née Olson) and her sister, Lena, kept house for their uncle Joe Gull, the superintendent. He said they were always of the opinion that the real target of the two bandits was Gull, and only through a lucky fluke was he not killed instead of Breckinridge. I asked them the obvious question: did Banty have blue eyes and light brown hair or blond hair. I awaited their return correspondence with great anticipation.

Their answer, when it came, was to the contrary: Coyote Bill's eyes were dark and his hair black. I had lost count of how many strikes that made against me, but in my own mind, I was a long way from being out.

As for the ultimate fate of Bill Banty, there are a number of theories, one of which was provided to me by Ed Asp of Dease Lake, British Columbia. I was showing him a number of photos I had of Albert Johnson when he spotted the photo of Banty.

He said: "How'd you get a picture of Bill *Elder*?" He explained that Elder journeyed into the Cassiar (Dease Lake country) in the thirties where he was a packer and horse wrangler. He died in a cave-in in a mine he was working alone in the forties.

Dease Lake, a place isolated from the rest of the world until the Cassiar Highway was built in the 1960s, would have been a logical place for a man like Bill Banty to flee.

In the spring of 1977, I visited the Craters of the Moon National Monument and told the staff there about Bill Banty and my research. This interested them, since a skeleton had been found in one of the caves but never identified. Was it Coyote Bill? It seems unlikely in view of the facts presented, but I suppose we will never know for sure.

CHAPTER 6

THE MYSTERIOUS DISAPPEARANCE OF ZANE GREY'S GUIDE

A S MY SEARCH CONTINUED, I was well aware that the Mad Trapper case had been publicized in just about every popular medium—television, magazines, newspapers, radio broadcasts, and even movies—all with no one coming forward to conclusively tear aside the veil of mystery that concealed Albert Johnson's true identity. I decided at last that *I* should try the national media. The most logical place to run a story on Johnson was a nature magazine like *Fur, Fish and Game*. This periodical had a wide circulation among outdoorsmen in both Canada and the United States. If further leads were ever going to appear, this seemed to be the best method of eliciting them. I wrote a short piece about Johnson in which I requested information, and included his death photo with the article. *Fur, Fish and Game* bought the story and I sat back and awaited results.

Clues were few in coming and of those that did come I felt only one was worth following up. This came from a man named Joe Byerhof of Elburn, Illinois. He wrote that between the years 1913 and 1915—he was not sure which—a Swede by the name of Pete Peterson had worked in a blacksmith shop in Kaneville, Illinois. Byerhof said he was there about three months when two detectives came over from Sweden and took him back to stand trial for murder. The story was that he had knifed a man who later died. Stated Byerhof, "I remember him and the description of the man in the story could be the same man."

I did everything I could to run down this lead including

dispatching letters to county, state, and federal authorities, with no luck. I wrote back to Byerhof and sent him a copy of my first book on Albert Johnson, but never heard from him again. Since Byerhof was in his seventies when he wrote, he may have passed away. One interesting fact about the story aside from the violent aspects was Peterson's association with blacksmithing. Albert Johnson had cut down the barrel of his 16-gauge shotgun to make a short gun out of it. Some skill is needed in doing this, and experience in blacksmithing would be of considerable help in any such endeavours as moulding a gun.

In any case, with Byerhof's silence, I had to lay that lead aside. If anything developed, it would be a point of reference which could be of value.

Another lead arose from the *Fur, Fish and Game* article, and it was verbal rather than written. I was having a beer in the Red Dog Saloon in Juneau, Alaska, when one of my fellow worthies at the bar, a man who happened to trap part-time, said he had read my article, and asked if I had ever read Zane Grey's books. Grey was a prolific producer of westerns, and one of the most popular writers of his day, from the early 1900s into the thirties. I said I had read some of them. He told me Zane Grey had once employed a guide who disappeared under strange circumstances. He could not recall much more about the man nor the year it happened, but he did remember one significant item: the man was Scandinavian.

When something happens concerning a famous author, there is always plenty of material about it. I searched through several of Grey's biographies and all of them discussed the individual my informant had spoken about. The guide was a Norwegian named Sivert Nielsen. The more I read about him, the more intrigued I became with his likeness to Albert Johnson.

Nielsen and Grey met as the result of a letter Nielsen wrote to Grey in 1915. He referred to having read one of Grey's books, *Desert Gold*, in which Grey mentioned a lost gold mine. Nielsen told Grey he had been prospecting since 1913 and had made four trips into the Sonora desert of Mexico, searching for minerals. Sivert proposed that an attempt be made to locate the lost mine Grey had written about, and if successful, that they split the treasure.

Grey was impressed by the letter, which was well-written, and wrote back to Nielsen explaining that the lost mine was only a figment of his imagination and the story was fiction. However, he invited Nielsen to visit him at his home in Avalon on Catalina Island off the California coast. Nielsen accepted the invitation, and Zane Grey was impressed by the man. He described Nielsen as thirty-five, of magnificent physique, weighing about 190 pounds, with shoulders so broad that he did not look as tall as his five feet ten inches.

Shortly after their meeting, Nielsen joined Grey on several fishing trips, forerunners of the many Grey was eventually to make in establishing himself as the top sports fisherman in the world at that time. Nielsen became a regular guide for Grey after these first casual trips.

Grey related some of the adventures of the Norwegian in his book *Tales of Lonely Trails*. He described Nielsen's travels while prospecting along Mexico's west coast, and how he avoided the dreaded Seri Indians. The Seris were known to have killed prospectors who ranged into their territory. Nielsen would wait for a low tide and walk the beach at night so a rising sea would wash away his tracks. Sometimes the Seris fired poisoned arrows, and on other occasions they even poisoned water holes. Illustrating their primitive state, Nielsen recalled once watching them from a hiding place as they tore apart and devoured a turtle raw.

In another adventure related by Grey, his guide was prospecting in the desert when a cougar killed his burro. As a consequence, he walked 150 miles to safety in three days, travelling as light as possible with nothing but a canteen of water and a few biscuits. Nielsen's stamina, his ability to live off the land, and even his name were similar to those the Mad Trapper used, Johnson having adapted them at different times to "Albert" and "Nelson". The parallel to Albert Johnson boosted my energy. A photo in one of Grey's books was enough like the photo of Johnson to fuel my interest further.

Zane Grey's guide Sivert Nielsen on the rim of the Tonto Basin in Arizona. SEEBURG FAMILY

The circumstances of Sivert's disappearance in 1924 were intriguing. Nielsen had written to Grey about a lost gold mine he knew of that he thought he could find if Grey would sponsor an expedition to look for it. Grey agreed to do this, but first went on a fishing trip to the east coast. When he returned west, he tried to contact Nielsen, but could not find him. The man had vanished.

Grey hired private detectives to see if they could turn up any clue as to his disappearance. They traced him to Tijuana, Mexico, a small border town just across the line from California. Here the trail ended. The sleuths reported a man answering Nielsen's description had been killed by revolutionaries in an insurrection in Baja California, but this was all they could find out.

Nielsen stepped out of Grey's life in 1924, the same year as the Goldpan Creek gold rush to Dease Lake, British Columbia, where Albert Johnson was reported to have been. This offered the possibility that the two men could be one and the same person.

Figuring that the right place to track Nielsen was Norway, I wrote to *Aftenposten*, Oslo's largest newspaper, seeking information about him. My letter was published; i.e. in a short time I received a letter from Elizabeth Seeberg, and at one stroke the fifty-year-old mystery was solved. She said Nielsen was a great-uncle of hers, and that he had died August 8, 1960 at the Meling Ranch in Baja California, where he had worked as a guide for many years. Why he had deserted Grey without notice she was unable to say.

So another lead had disintegrated. I passed the information about Nielsen along to Grey's sons, Romer and Loren, explaining that Nielsen had settled at the Meling Ranch—not only working as a guide but prospecting and mining for the entire period from 1924 to 1960. They expressed considerable interest in my continuing search for Albert Johnson's identity and thanked me for informing them about a man they had both admired as youngsters. Loren added that if I ever located Sivert's lost mine I should let him know. I promised that I would—after I staked my claim.

CHAPTER 7

THE ECCENTRIC CARPENTER FROM ANYOX

A S MY RESEARCH CONTINUED without the hoped-for result, fatigue began to set in, and a certain sense of futility. I
had devoted almost all my spare time for years to this enigma,
incurred expenses and travelled far afield. Had learned, perhaps, something about human nature, too. But while solving a
mystery was a creditable goal, it was not one to be pursued
endlessly. I decided on one last fling at identifying Johnson.

One of the statements Albert Johnson made to Roy Buttle at
Ross River was that he had once worked at the Anyox Mine in
northern British Columbia. That operation was long since shut
down, but it was a clue that begged for examination. I was able
to find the employment records intact at the Granby Mine near
Grand Forks, B.C., 500 miles away from the Anyox location.

I went to Grand Forks where mine superintendent Boyd
Hardwicke considerately let me look at the fifty-year-old personnel file where the dust was thicker than sand in a Sahara
windstorm. I almost literally choked on the records.

While examining personnel cards I tried to imagine what
aliases Albert Johnson might have taken besides the name
Arthur Nelson, as there were no employees in the correct time
period listed under either name. Some of the cards contained
physical descriptions which narrowed the choice by several
hundreds, but the sifting was still a big job. It was an interesting
dip into the past, but also somewhat saddening when I realized
that most of the men whose records I lightly flipped through
had already passed on. The nostalgia evoked by it all seemed to

exaggerate the fragility of life, and also its futility. We are really but grains of sand in the winds of time.

I wrote down a number of names to trace as best I could. They included: John Bakketon, twenty-three in 1925, mucker, whose father was from Voss, Norway; Arthur Isaksson, twenty-nine in 1924, from Malberget, Sweden; Mike Nykolichuk, twenty-five in 1920, mucker, American, whose brother Nick worked at the Cassidy coal mine in Wayne, Alberta; John Nelson, twenty-eight, Dane, whose brother Nels also worked at the Cassidy mine; A. Nilsen, who was thirty-eight in 1925, no home town given; and Pete Peterson, thirty-seven, carpenter, from Langasjo, Sweden.

I felt the most likely leads among the men on the list were Bakketon and Isaksson. By now I was catching on to the quickest way of tracking down anyone in Scandinavia and that was by first writing directly to the parish of the community from which the immigrant came, and if that failed, by writing to the Salvation Army. I usually mailed a small donation to the latter along with my request. If the Salvation Army was stumped, I would send a letter to the newspaper of the community involved.

Through Salvation Army headquarters in Oslo, Norway, I obtained the address of a sister of John Bakketon. She answered my query in her own language. I rounded up a Norwegian to translate it for me and learned that Bakketon had died of industrial poisoning at a mine in British Columbia in 1939. That cancelled that lead.

I wrote to the parish in Malberget in search of Arthur Isaksson, and found out he had once worked in the iron mine there but the parish people did not know what had happened to him after that. Through writing further letters I received one item that seemed relevant. Isaksson had emigrated to British Columbia, and his wife had died on the way to join him there later. Lesser setbacks than that have sent a man off the "deep end". More letters turned up information that Isaksson had returned to Sweden on hearing of his wife's death and had settled near the city of Kiruna. He passed away only a few months before my query arrived. This troubled me because I felt that even if none of the men whose names I had was Johnson, the discovery that one of them had known him or been a fellow immigrant would itself have been valuable.

I turned my attention to Pete Peterson. Though thirty-seven in 1923, a little old in light of Johnson's projected age, his description fitted that of the trapper. His having been a carpenter on the Anyox New Railroad (a spur from the mine to the docks at tidewater) fit well with Johnson's ability to build cabins in the bush with a minimum of tools. I wrote to Langasjo, Sweden, and obtained the address of his brother from the parish registry. I then wrote to his brother: he did not know what had happened to him. He said, though, that Pete Peterson's real name was Per August Eliasson. These two points were encouraging, in that Pete took an assumed name and had never told his kin where he was. (The trapper's cabin had contained no clues of familial connections whatever.)

He also sent me a photo of Peterson, and one look at it made me wonder if, at long last, I might have found a hot lead: there was a resemblance between Peterson and Albert Johnson. Both had fair hair, large nostrils, and ears and eyes similarly set. Of particular interest to me was an enlarged pupil of Peterson's right eye which could indicate an illness. At his death Albert Johnson had in his possession thirty-two kidney pills. I sent Peterson's photo to an eye doctor and he said the enlarged pupil could reflect a range of different disorders including an injury to the back of the head, a pituitary tumour in the brain, carcinoma of the lungs, an eye injury, or infection of the kidneys. The latter not only jibed with the kidney pills in Johnson's possession but also with the fact that Arthur Nelson had purchased a year's supply of kidney pills from the Taylor and Drury store in Mayo in the spring of 1931.

I wrote to Canadian Immigration and the walls I was carefully constructing came tumbling down in a hurry. They told me Peterson died in a hospital in Vancouver. I contacted the records section there and they added that the year of death was 1934, a full two years after Albert Johnson's demise.

Doggedly, onward. Regarding the Nykolichuk brothers (and the rumour that Johnson may have been called "Mick" or "Nick"), I wrote to the North Dakota Archives and found a family recorded in the 1915 census, but no one known by that nickname. The research was such a long shot I dropped it completely. The same held true for the Nelson brothers. Their names were just too common for me to be able to follow them up with such limited information. Besides, their records and many others did not include physical descriptions.

The last name on my list was tantalizing although it could have been just one variation of many, but A. Nilsen had given no address as a reference, and his age made him somewhat doubtful as the trapper because he would have been forty-five in 1932. I did write for the list of Nilsens who served in the First World War from North Dakota, but there was no A. Nilsen.

I kept coming back to North Dakota as a base. When Johnson said he was from that state in his conversation with trader Roy Buttle, he probably felt safe in doing so and therefore may have told the truth. Since this was in context with other "truths" he related about Teslin and Dease Lake, and possibly the mine at Anyox, it was about the only thread I still had to follow.

A supplementary lead also pertained to Anyox, and was obtained from a book I had read about the mine, entitled *The Town That Got Lost* by Robert Loudon.[1] Loudon was born at Anyox and lived there for many years. When the mine closed his family moved away. Eventually he became a newspaper man. One day he opted to return to the community of his youth, which he did, and the result was the book. In it he generously gave credit to a man named Ozzie Hutchings as a source for much of the early history of Anyox from 1903 until it blossomed into a full-scale operation a decade later. I wrote to Loudon, who gave me Hutchings' address. Thus began a correspondence that lasted until Ozzie's death several years later.

I asked him if he had ever run into a person who would match my description of Albert Johnson. Hutchings answered that not only had he run into such a man but he had mentioned him in an unpublished manuscript he had written about Anyox. Hutchings said this man was very much a loner. Ozzie had been working in a gang repairing an old trestle bridge that carried water to the mining community when the new man arrived in the spring of 1923. In conversations with the newly arrived carpenter, Hutchings learned he was a Norwegian. Ozzie did not notice much of an accent, so the newcomer may have been a long time in North America. Though generally silent and withdrawn with the rest of the crew, he seemed to relax in Hutchings' presence. Ozzie figured the newcomer felt a certain kinship toward him because he himself looked like a Scandinavian, being blond and blue-eyed and nicknamed "Swede".

They had been working together for about a month when the loner approached Hutchings and told him he planned to hunt and trap in the interior of British Columbia the next winter. He said he understood that Ozzie had done the same and wondered if Hutchings would look at a sled he had built to carry his supplies. Hutchings agreed and inspected the sled after work one day. Hutchings said he politely pointed out that the sled would be too heavy. The Norwegian explained that he planned to buy a pony to pull it, and hence its size. Hutchings thought that a pony would be hard put to survive because of the ten-foot snows that piled up in the interior. He said a dog team would be better.

The stranger thanked him for his advice, but did not comment on whether or not he would accept it. Later he bought a 40-60 model 1876 Winchester from Ozzie, and in the fall went ahead and bought a pony about the size of a Shetland. He quit his job in November and, loading the pony, sled, and supplies on a boat he had purchased, set out across Observatory Inlet to the Nass River up which he travelled to the interior. That was the last Ozzie saw of him. I asked Hutchings if he could recall the name of his quiet friend and he could not. On receiving copies of four death photos of Albert Johnson that I mailed him, Hutchings said he thought the men looked similar but more so in the full-face portrait than in the others.

Assuming the man was Albert Johnson, several interesting points arose out of Hutchings' memoirs. Of considerable interest to me was his friend's route north. If he went up the Nass River and portaged, he would have encountered the Telegraph Trail, which ran 250 miles north to the town of Telegraph Creek. Along this trail was Echo Lake, where Albert Johnson was rumoured to have spent one winter. I was also interested in the man's desire to use a horse in winter, and his unfamiliarity with the country. Both points showed that Johnson was not from any place near that part of British Columbia. They also indicated there was a certain degree of illogical stubbornness on Johnson's part. This trait, though not an all-consuming one, was certainly a part of the trapper's make-up.

The Hutchings' reference was the last of my Anyox leads. If Ozzie could have recalled the man's name, I would have been able to cross-check it with personnel records. Even then, however, if Johnson were using an alias, it is doubtful that the information would have been traceable.

More importantly, though Hutchings' recollections tended to favour my theory that Johnson had told the truth about being from North Dakota, I was stumped once again. Running down leads through a mine where thousands of men had worked, where many were Scandinavians, was about as practical as going through a phone book looking for a man named Smith. I shelved the project and went fishing. Beautiful grayling pack the creeks during the Yukon spring, and the angling could not be more satisfying.

CHAPTER 8

THE "WRONG MAN" THEME

I T IS AMAZING how undocumented "hearsay" hangs on and on. One of the more prevalent rumours about the Albert Johnson case was the one that held that the Mounties killed the wrong man. Indeed, there was a real incident that had spawned this rumour and it flourished for half a century.

The story concerned a retired civil servant, Sam Kitchen, a friendly giant of a man who had seen many years of service in northern Alberta and the Northwest Territories. After retirement, his stature and ruggedly handsome countenance made him a natural to play the part of a frontiersman in a number of movies, one being *Saskatchewan*, starring Alan Ladd. In that movie Sam gunned down a buffalo before the cameras. Kitchen claimed he had known the Mad Trapper and even displayed a photograph to prove it. He was so certain that the person he had known was Albert Johnson of Rat River fame that he inscribed the desperado's name on the photo and donated it to the Alberta Archives.

Archives introduced me to Sam via the mails. I asked his permission to use the photo and he gave it. I asked where he had met the individual in the photo and he answered in Wisconsin. Other than this fact, Kitchen was vague about the man's name and the photo's origin. I filed the picture away with all the rest of the Mad Trapper memorabilia I had collected and forgot about it.

In the meantime, the "wrong man" premise gained momentum, and speculation on the theme grew like hydras' heads as I methodically cut off my leads. Apologists for this school of thought advanced the argument that the man who shot King got away, and an innocent individual had been seized by the long reach of the law, only to be chased down and killed. The only way such a mistake could have been made was for a stranger or an innocent partner to have occupied Johnson's cabin after Johnson shot Constable King, and to have been saddled with the rap after Johnson fled.

Adding weight to this theory was the fact that the RCMP never officially established Albert Johnson's identity. Since the Mounties did not know who the trapper was, how could they know that the slain man was the guilty one?

Compounding this confusion through the years was Kitchen displaying his photo and saying it was of Albert Johnson, the man killed by the Mounties. It seemed to me that the picture was nourishing the roots of the "wrong man" premise, and not doing my research any good.

Carefully reviewing the actual course of events of the Johnson trackdown, it can be seen that no mistake was made by the Mounties. They certainly killed the fractious character who shot King, whoever he was. The proof was written in the snow—the snowshoe tracks, the idiosyncrasies that could never fool experienced trackers in the north. The lawmen followed the trail of the character over the headwaters of the Rat and Barrier rivers to the Bell River, and then up the ice of the Eagle, a snake-shaped tributary that drained southward into the Bell. To ensure that the posse did not make a mistake they were told that two men—Bill Anderson and Phil Branstrom—were trapping far up the Eagle River.

The Mounties caught up with Albert Johnson twenty-five miles up the Eagle River, engaged the fugitive in a fierce gunfight, and killed him. Next to his bullet-torn body were crudely-made snowshoes, the distinctive print of which the posse had followed for five weeks.

So where did the Kitchen photo come in? My first break in that direction came when an acquaintance of mine, George Clark, who lived for many years in Inuvik and Fort McPherson, talked with an elderly gent whose trap line had spanned part of the area where the chase took place. Clark had a copy of Kitchen's photo and showed it to the old man, who immediately recognized the man in it, who, he said, was trapping on the Eagle River at the time Johnson was killed. However, he could not recall the trapper's name.

As soon as Clark related the above information to me, I was able to fill in the rest of it: the man of the photo had to be either Anderson or Branstrom, since they were the only people on the Eagle that winter. By sheer good fortune, I knew a former trapper, Paul Nieman, who had been on the Bell River not far from the Eagle on the day Johnson was killed.

I assumed that he would more than likely know his counterparts trapping on the Eagle. I took the Kitchen photo over to him. He scanned it and announced that the man in it was Phil Branstrom. I asked him what had happened to him. Nieman said Branstrom left the Eagle River that spring because of an ulcer that acted up, and he had never returned. Paul figured he went to Vancouver for treatment but he was not sure.

Suddenly, it was easy to see how the "wrong man" theory was perpetuated by the Kitchen photo. Sam Kitchen thought the man in his photo was Albert Johnson (though, in fact, it was Phil Branstrom). When Kitchen saw that it was not Branstrom who was shot on the Eagle River, he concluded that the Mounties shot the wrong man! And indeed Branstrom did "disappear" from the north—down to Vancouver for treatment.

But Branstrom, of course, was nowhere near Albert Johnson's Rat River cabin when King was shot, launching the manhunt, and so he could not have been the Mad Trapper.

Like so many other leads, this one too had come to nothing. I suppose that this was at least partial success—I kept proving that So-and-so was *not* the Mad Trapper. But so far I had been totally unsuccessful in proving that someone—a man with a real history and a background—*was* the man known as Albert Johnson.

In a way, every one of the dozens of clues I had meticulously

Phil Branstrom trapped at a lake a few miles west of the Eagle River where the Mad Trapper was shot, and was for years mistaken for Albert Johnson. PROVINCIAL ARCHIVES OF ALBERTA, A2173

followed for years was simply a variation on the "wrong man" theme—a refrain that no one had been able to round out in the fifty years since that strangely inconclusive shoot-out on the Eagle River.

PART TWO

A NORTHERN LEGACY OF THE WILD WEST

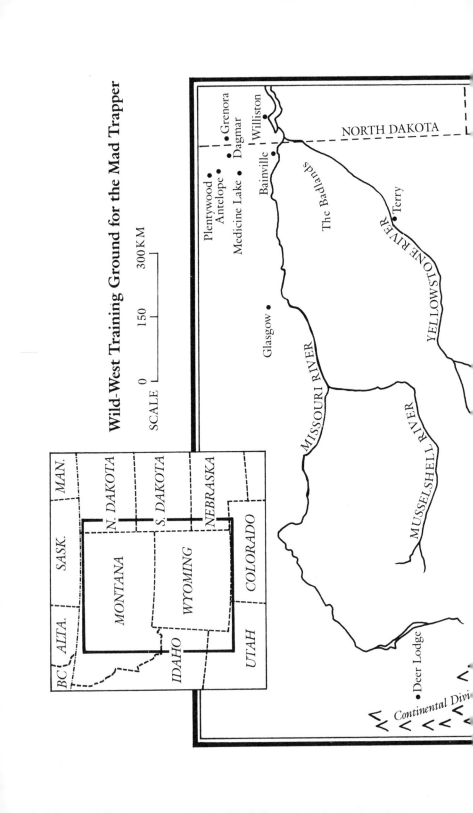

Wild-West Training Ground for the Mad Trapper

SCALE
0   150   300 KM

Plentywood
Antelope
Medicine Lake
Grenora
Dagmar
Williston
Bainville

NORTH DAKOTA

Glasgow

The Badlands

MISSOURI RIVER

YELLOWSTONE RIVER

Terry

MUSSELSHELL RIVER

Deer Lodge

Continental Divi

BC   ALTA.   SASK.   MAN.

N. DAKOTA

S. DAKOTA

MONTANA

WYOMING

NEBRASKA

IDAHO

UTAH   COLORADO

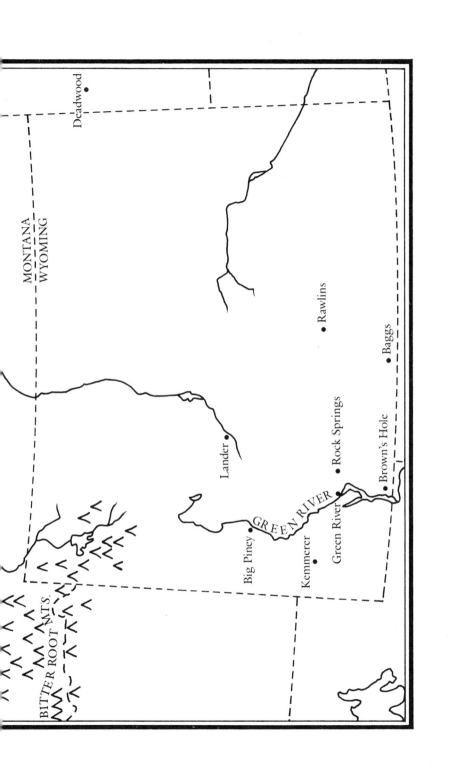

CHAPTER 9

THE BADLANDS
IMMIGRANTS

I HAD TRIED TO CRACK the Dakota hunch for four years; then one day "Dakota" came to me. Katherine Bauman of North Dakota's State Historical Society answered my query of several years earlier. She sent me a letter in which she enclosed photocopies of several pages from an article written by Wallace Rustad in an obscure history of Williams County, published by the county. This article put forth the theory that a North Dakota man by the name of Johnny Johnson was Albert Johnson, the "Mad Trapper of Rat River".

I was becoming jaded with accounts that ended up as blind leads, but I could not afford to ignore anything coming from North Dakota. Impatiently scanning Rustad's article, I came across an item that leaped at me, a reference to a daring bank robbery staged by John and his half-brother, Magnor Hanson, in 1915. In a gun battle that followed, Magnor had been wounded and captured, but Johnny had escaped.

Rustad's article was based on a term paper he had written as a history-course requirement at the University of North Dakota at Minot in 1962, and I obtained a copy of it. I recalled a statement once made to me by Tom Sturgeon, another old Yukoner I had interviewed in years past about Albert Johnson having been a cowboy from the American West. I read the paper carefully.

And I compared his research with my own. Rustad postulated that Johnny and Albert were one and the same. His hunch was based on his viewing of the death photo, probably in the same detective magazine that so many others had seen, but his proof was limited. He had checked with the Mounties in Regina, but they could not answer his questions. In the research business you can never take anything for granted, especially anything from "secondary sources". I wrote to the Williams County Historical Society and obtained Rustad's address. I also ordered volume I of the Williams County History. It is an incredibly detailed documentation of the history of the county through the memories of each family who lived there, and consists of 940 8½ x 11-inch pages.

On August 3, 1979, I contacted Rustad by phone and he said to date he had no reason to believe his thesis was incorrect. In other words, no information had surfaced through the years to prove that John was not Albert. Lack of negative evidence is not the same as *positive* evidence, of course, but he seemed quite confident of his results.

Subsequent research revealed that Rustad had erred in a few points, such as the date of the Johnson family's emigration, but all in all, he had done some good legwork.

Rustad wrote that the Johnson family had emigrated to North Dakota from Norway in 1899, and gave the age of John as one that year. The exact date of birth is of considerable aid in tracing an individual so I wrote to the Williams County Court and the clerk replied that Johnny was born in *1899*, not *1898*. To straighten out the record once and for all, I appealed to the Salvation Army in Norway, which sent me a copy of Johnson's birth certificate. He was born John Konrad Jonsen on July 13, 1898, in Bardu, Norway, a small town situated 180 miles north of the Arctic Circle in Nordlands province. Johnny's mother, Petra (née Freddrikke Johansdatter), was born in Målselv, Norway, in 1861, and his father, Anders Gustaf Jonsen,[1] in Flen, Sweden, about fifty miles west of Stockholm, on June 24, 1848. (Recall that Albert Johnson had told different people in the Yukon and British Columbia at various times that he was both Swedish and Norwegian and, on one occasion, Danish. The fact that his father was Swedish and his mother Norwegian would make sense of that apparent contradiction!) Others in the

DEN NORSKE KIRKE

Dåpsattest

	slektsnavn	
For guttpike	Jonsen	
	fornavn og ev. mellomnavn	
	Johan Konrad	
Født	dato og år	13/7 1898 -trettende juli a.h.nittiåtte-
	i	Bardu
Døpt	dato og år	30/10 1898 -trettiende oktober a-h-nittiåtte-
	i	Bardu
Foreldre (dersom vedk. er adoptert skal adoptiv-foreldrene føres opp som foreldre)		Anders Gustav Jonsen
		og h-Petra Fredrikke Johansdatter
Attesten er utskrift av kirkeboka for	sokn	Bardu
	by/prestegjeld	Bardu

Bardu sokneprest - embete, den 7-juni 19 79

Johan Flekstad
underskrift

F-107

The baptismal certificate for Johan Konrad Jonsen (Johnny Johnson), who was born of mixed Swedish/Norwegian parentage in Bardu, Norway in 1898. SOKNEPREST/J. FLEKSTAD

family, all born in Bardu, were: Magnor Hansen, born September 7, 1892 (spelled "Hanson" after he came to the United States); Helga, March 16, 1894; Sina (Signe), April 13, 1895; and Olaga (Olga), June 3, 1902.

John's father was a stable-boy as a youth and later became a carriage driver and blacksmith for a wealthy Swedish family. While in his thirties he emigrated to Norway and married Petra. Since most of the people around Bardu were farmers, presumably Andrew pursued the same occupation. *Bardu* is a Laplander word meaning "resting place". Laplanders who drove their giant herds of reindeer to Norway's coast in the summers would make camp at the pleasant dell that makes up Bardu, and gave it its name.

Times were difficult in Scandinavia in the 1880s and early 1900s. Land was scarce and almost impossible to obtain, even after a lifetime of toil. Consequently, Anders was not averse to publicity tracts released by American railroads luring immigrants to settle on "free" homesteads in the "beautiful" American West.

Free land was better than no land at all, so the Johnsons decided to emigrate and sailed from Christiana (now Oslo), Norway, aboard the *United States* on July 15, 1904, when Johnny was six years old. Their ship docked in New York, and shortly thereafter the Johnsons cleared customs and rode west aboard an immigrant train. Anders spent a month in Minnesota, did not like it, and moved on to North Dakota, where he obtained a homestead of 320 waterless, woodless, and rattlesnake-infested acres, just north of the infamous Dakota "badlands". What Anders and Petra thought when they saw this treeless expanse of nothingness would be interesting compared to the picturesque fjords, mountains, and forest-covered country they had left. If they had packed up and turned around and gone immediately back to the "old country" they certainly could have been forgiven, but it took money to do that, something they did not have—or they probably never would have emigrated in the first place.

Andrew Johnson was no starry-eyed youth looking for the pot of gold at the end of the rainbow. He was fifty-seven years old. He could not speak English nor could his wife, and at that age he probably would never learn it unless he had an exceptional facility in languages. This was a disadvantage to them, but it was tempered somewhat by the presence of thousands of other Scandinavians building shacks in the same area as the Johnsons. At least he could converse with them.

Owing to this language problem, Andrew's and Petra's offspring became unofficial interpreters. Children do not have the built-in resistance to learning a new language that often impedes older people. Often in such cases, too, a youngster still speaking the foreign language daily with his parents, cannot shake the vestiges of his home country's accent even while he or she is learning English. A perfect example of this was a seventy-year-old Laplander named Andy Bangs whom I once interviewed in Unalakleet, Alaska. Andy talked with a Norwegian accent although he was born in Alaska and had never seen

Norway. His parents were reindeer herders from the town of Kautokeino, Norway, and presumably they, like Johnson's parents, never learned English.

The significance of this stress on language is obvious. The man Johnny may have been, Albert Johnson, spoke with a *slight* Scandinavian accent, at least according to those people who met him in the Northwest Territories and the Yukon Territory.

According to Rustad's research, Andrew apparently tried to learn English by inviting a teacher, Hyder Poling, to live at the farm. Poling was also installed to hold regular classes for the Johnson children and others in the area. This lasted for only a few weeks before the instructor returned to his own farm and held classes there.

The Williams County history illustrated that life for a youth on the western plains was one of continuous toil, especially for those children whose families were financially impoverished before they ever ploughed a furrow. Most of the immigrants fell into this category, and at first they lived in tents or lean-tos until they put together sod houses and finally wood-frame structures.

Coming from Norway, where wood and water were in abundance, to a place like western North Dakota, where there wasn't much of either, must have been a tremendous shock. The Johnsons had to trek forty miles to the Missouri River valley to get wood. Long trips were also necessary to fetch water. Scattered buffalo chips (though the bison themselves were long gone) provided fuel, until coal was discovered.

The winters were bitterly cold. Storms swept in from the north with the velocity of hurricanes, driving residents into their homes for days at a time; they did not dare to step out for fear of becoming lost twenty yards from their own front doors. Ropes had to be strung from the house to the barn and sometimes tunnels were dug when the snow became roof-high. It seemed that whenever a farmer got a little ahead, a natural disaster like a blizzard came along to wipe out his crops or cattle. In the summer, the farmer had to contend with the lack of rain that withered and killed his crops. If he was one of the few who managed to irrigate, great prairie fires could still burn out a decade's toil in a matter of minutes. Other natural dangers like flash floods and tornadoes could suddenly deprive a man not only of his ability to make a living but of his life as well.

A boy raised in this environment was toughened to the outdoor life by the very fact of his existence because that's where he spent fourteen to sixteen hours of each day—outdoors, haying, planting, herding cattle and horses, cutting grain, milking cows, harvesting crops of all kinds, going to school when he had time, and hunting and trapping.

Like many of the boys raised in the same circumstances Johnny learned the rudiments of trapping, but would not be considered a knowledgeable trapper in the eyes of the men of the veteran fur brigades like the Hudson's Bay Company or the North West Company and others who had tramped through the region a century before. The know-how needed to harvest the wolf, wolverine, marten and ermine would have to be learned elsewhere. As a young lad, Johnny trapped muskrats, foxes, and an occasional otter. These pelts were enough to give him a little pocket money now and then.

Rustad's paper noted that Johnson was given a rifle almost as soon as he could hold one. Any food he could shoot for the table was of that much more help to feed a family of seven. He hunted everything edible on the plains, from rabbits and gophers to deer and antelope, and in so doing became a crack shot. Guns became a way of life to him, and he became so expert at shooting with a rifle that he could be called an "intuitive" shooter, meaning he raised and fired the rifle all in one movement without seeming to aim. His ability may have been "aided" by an accident when the flick of a bull whip struck him and permanently injured his left eye. By losing part of his sight in that eye, he may have been forced to concentrate even more on perfecting his skill. Johnny also became expert with heavy calibre revolvers. He was able to shoot the head off a rattlesnake at twenty yards firing from either hand, and crows on the wing at one hundred yards with a rifle.

Almost as soon as John learned to shoot, he also began to ride, and before long he and Magnor were operating a business of their father's, breaking horses to the saddle and the plough. Busting broncs was no easy way to earn a living and it made the boys into better-than-average riders and appraisers of horse flesh. Rustad pointed out that they became friendly with one Bert Delker, whose real name was Martinus B. Mortenson, through this work.

Born in Denmark in 1875, Delker was a tall, handsome man with a pencil-thin moustache and a bearing that suggested a certain imperiousness and an inner fibre common to men who had ridden the "owl hoot" trail. The fact that Delker packed a .44 revolver on his hip everywhere he went added to this image. Delker lived in a sod house a quarter of a mile across the road and down a coulee from the Johnson farm. He ran cattle on his section, but his first love was horses. Delker had connections from North Dakota clear down through the badlands to Deadwood, South Dakota, through which he dealt for ponies that were obtained in ways beyond the law. His acquaintances included Kji Mathews, also a Dane, who lived near Bainville, Montana, and who also operated on the fringes of the law buying and selling rustled horses that were fed into a "pipeline" conveying the animals to Canadian markets. (Delker was a horse thief, albeit a cautious one, and for a good reason that Rustad did not list. I journeyed to Montana Archives and found out: he had served from 1906 to 1910 in the Montana State Penitentiary at Deer Lodge, having been convicted of rustling horses near Glasgow, Montana.)

From scanning Delker's prison record at the Montana Archives, I concluded there was a possibility that Bert Delker had at one time or another been a member of the infamous Wild Bunch. This gang of long riders was at times led by either Butch Cassidy or Harvey Logan (a.k.a. "Kid" Curry) and was known for its depredations against trains and banks at the turn of the century. The fact that Delker listed his sister, Mrs. Hannah Hejde, as living in Lander, Wyoming, an area included in the Rock Springs–Baggs–Green River triangle which was a supply and recreational point for the "Bunch", lends credit to this supposition. As far as the fortunes of the elder Johnsons were concerned, there could not have been a worse neighbour.

For two boys who loved horses, and lived on a poverty-ridden farm like Johnny and Magnor, Delker drew them like a magnet. The gunman, despite his stern posture, was not unlikeable, and had helped others in need. On one occasion he was visiting neighbours who apologized for not having cream for coffee. The next day Bert brought a cow and a calf which he gave to them, asking nothing in return.

Young John began to spend more time with the cowboy as he got older. Delker had married John's sister Signe in 1912, but she died in childbirth the next year. Shortly afterwards Johnny left home and moved in with his pistol-packing neighbour. During this period John honed his ability with six-guns to a fine edge.

Parallel to Johnny's coming-of-age, and his leaving home, he developed another interest: girls. At the age of fifteen John became enamoured of a girl named Thora Hermanson, also an immigrant child whose widowed mother came from Norway. John spent many pleasant hours with her riding horses, on picnics, going to an occasional square dance and trading presents on birthdays and at Christmas. As most youngsters discover at the age of fifteen or thereabouts, sooner or later the need for cash raises its ugly head. If John wanted to bestow gifts on Thora's lovely head, he soon realized it took money to purchase it and that was something he did not have. Some lads corrected this situation by working extra hours off the farm, or by selling a horse or other animal they had personally raised. In John's case another solution somewhat less respectable but much more adventurous was to present itself.

This "gambol" as Rustad reported it, was said to have arisen from a suggestion by Delker. But knowing that youngsters are prone to cast blame on everyone but themselves in such cases, it is impossible at this late date to determine for sure who was the moving force behind the plan to hold up the Farmers' State Bank of Medicine Lake, Montana.

Word had come to Delker that the bank was maintaining a heavy cash position and would be a logical choice to divest of its funds. The three planned the robbery, or at least Magnor and John planned it with help from the older man, though the latter

Main Street, Medicine Lake, Montana, circa 1915. The Farmers'
State Bank is directly behind the two people walking together at
left. BELL BROS./MONTANA STATE HISTORICAL SOCIETY

was not to take an active role other than to supply the horses.
Filling in gaps in Rustad's story with my own research among
prison records and newspapers, and by corresponding with
residents from that area still alive, I was able to come up with the
sequence of steps that was to lead Johnny in a downward spiral
from which he never escaped.

Because of Johnny's youth, his older brother and Delker
decided that they should rob a hardware store in Bainville,
Montana, as the test of John's nerve. Not only did Johnny pass
the "exam", he managed it with a twist of which even Butch
Cassidy would have been proud. John asked the proprietor,
Louis Haefner, if he would load a gun John said he wanted to
buy. Haefner did this, passing the revolver to Johnny, who then
held him up with it. This was more fun than school!

On February 11, 1915, John and Magnor proceeded to
Medicine Lake, and held up the Farmers' State Bank, using four

guns between them to persuade the bankers that they meant business. The irony here was that the bank's vice-president, H. G. Anderson, and the cashier, S. C. Faaborg, were both personally acquainted with the lads and had even invited them into the back room to have coffee and warm up prior to the bank opening officially for business. Johnny and Magnor sipped coffee with them, and as soon as the cashier opened the vault Magnor stuck two six-guns into his gut and told him he wanted the money. At first the cashier figured it was a prank, but when both lads cocked their guns and announced that it was not, the man handed the cash over to them. This amounted to over $2,800, more money than Magnor and Johnny and most of the residents of North Dakota had ever seen at one time in their lives.

The brothers tied up the bankers with their own suspenders and walked out of the bank. They mounted their horses, and as nonchalantly as possible under the circumstances eased out of town to avoid suspicion and then put the animals into a canter.

One of the victims soon freed himself of his bonds and called the sheriff. The chase was on, but a chase in 1915 was different from one of twenty years earlier. The telephone now made it acutely difficult for would-be bandits to escape. The sheriff, John Duggan, once he had determined the direction in which the boys were riding, simply called ahead to his colleague, Sheriff Grossgard of the town of Dagmar, and asked that a posse be formed to stop them. This was done, and about ten miles out, Magnor and Johnny ran head-on into a phalanx of ranchers stretched across the road. The boys were ordered to surrender, but instead they charged directly toward the enemy lines and broke through the surprised cordon of men. The youths had passed that obstacle successfully when a rifle shot ripped through Magnor's shoulder and he collapsed on his horse's neck, still riding. He managed to pass most of the money to John before falling to the ground in a heap near the Lovejoy farm, several miles east of where he was hit.

John rode five or six more miles before the posse caught up with him at the North Dakota state line. Here, six or seven men arrayed against him, John fought them off from the sanctuary of a rock pile. Both sheriffs were well aware of Johnny's reputation with a revolver, and they instructed their men not to expose themselves to his unerring aim. Johnny did so well that he kept the posse pinned down, and then escaped under a cover of fog that rolled in.

Once he broke away from his siege with the posse, Johnson coolly stopped at a farm owned by someone named Gilbertson, bought a fast horse, and then bolted for Delker's place. Bert provided him with supplies, a fresh horse, and suggested he ride for Ki Mathews' ranch near Bainville. Johnson did this and, somewhat miraculously, since he was well known by most of the people in the area, again escaped the clutches of the law.

Mathews relayed him to another "sympathizer" named Peterson who took him, his horse, and outfit by wagon through Bainville and down to the valley bottom of the Missouri River. Stopped by a deputy sheriff along the way, Peterson and the boy said they were going to cut wood. When they were out of sight of Bainville, the lad saddled up his horse, crossed the Missouri River ice and holed up in a vacant schoolhouse during a four-day blizzard, after which he headed west.[2]

CHAPTER 10

ON THE TRAIL OF A WYOMING HORSE THIEF

THE DARING HOLD-UP shook Sheridan and Williams counties to their roots. Notoriety came to the Johnson family quickly, compliments of the news media. Associated Press hammered out the story on their news wire and it hit most of the front pages of the nation's newspapers. The Seattle *Times* for example, under a front page dateline on February 12, 1915, wrote: "Bound fast in their chairs with suspenders, the cashier and assistant of the Farmers' State Bank of Medicine Lake, Montana, were compelled to witness masked robbers loot the bank of $2,500 in cash. . . ." Two days later the wire service published the story of Magnor Hanson's capture, including his having been shot out of the saddle by a posse. At the same time, it reported, erroneously, that Johnny Johnson had been arrested.

Newspaper coverage of the hold-up, though somewhat lacking in accuracy, was certainly not wanting in enthusiasm. It culminated in a rip-roaring, journalistic free-for-all in which charges, insinuations, and insults were hurled about with abandon. At the centre of this storm was Sheriff Jack Duggan of Montana's Sheridan County, who was charged with the responsibility of capturing Johnny and whose competence was in question. His ears probably burned with the same intensity that Inspector Eames' ears were to burn seventeen years later, and the embarrassment of the county sheriff's office was no doubt equal to that of the Mounties who found it necessary to call out everything but the Royal Navy to apprehend Albert Johnson.

The parallels between the two events, from Johnny's "miraculous" escape while surrounded, down to the press-circus news coverage, present, in retrospect, an intriguing similarity.

The very brazenness of the 1915 hold-up captured the imagination of the public, and since it occurred on the Thursday morning—the day most weekly journals publish—the local press played it up for all it was worth. As a consequence of the headlong rush to get into print, editorial blunders were the order of the day. Again this was not unlike the "Arctic Circle War" of 1932 during which one newspaper published a photo of the "Mad Trapper" Albert Johnson only to have the real subject of the photo come storming into the editorial room screaming for a retraction. He was Albert Johnson all right, and also a trapper, but definitely not a madman gunning down Mounties in the far north.

When a newspaper or wire service stumbles over its lines, the goof is impossible to disguise, making the perpetrator of the mistake fair game for those publications in competition with it. After the 1915 bank hold-up, Associated Press beat the local news media in reporting the picaresque fact that the victim's own suspenders had been used to tie them up during the crime, and in so doing put Medicine Lake scribes on tenterhooks waiting for the giant news service to trip over some other fact or bit of shoddy journalism. It was not long in coming. When, a few days later, AP reported John's arrest when actually the sixteen-year-old was still dodging posses as though born to the art, the AP man refused to run a correction and let the whole story die. Since in that part of the country sheriffs were elected and campaigned for the job, the lawman's competence (or lack of it) became a political football, too.

The journalistic joust was initiated by Mr. Nelson, editor of the Plentywood *Herald*, who charged that Editor Doolin of the Medicine Lake *Wave* and the two bankers were scared out of their socks by the robbers. Doolin, whose Irish sense of humour deserted him after this attack on his courage, lambasted the *Herald*, and levelled another cannonade at the Sheridan County *News*, for copying the *Wave*'s coverage word by

BANK ROBBED AT 9:45 THURSDAY MORNING.

ROBBERS MAKE A DARING GET-A-WAY WITH BOODLE OF NEARLY $3,000.00

One of the most daring bank robberies ever staged in this section of Montana was pulled off here this (Thursday) morning shortly after the opening of the Farmers Bank. While Vice-President H. G. Anderson and Cashier S. C. Faaborg were both in the bank this morning at about 9:45 two young men entered the bank and ordered them to 'throw up their hands'. It came as a surprise to both gentlemen and for a moment they thought the order merely a joke but upon the appearance of four large caliber six shooters, one in each hand of the robbers they quickly changed their minds and complied with the request, when the younger of the robbers proceeded to tie their hands behind their backs.

While the elder of the two robbers kept them 'covered' the youngest who is but seventeen years of age proceeded to the vault and helped himself to something over $2800.-00 which he hurriedly pushed into a sack and the two backed out the door and made their way to their saddle horses which were tied near the Stubban store and galloped out of town.

Mr. Faaborg succeeded in getting his hands free and released Mr. Anderson who immediately called Sheriff Duggan who happened to be in town and accompanied by J. M. Leonard started in hasty pursuit. Alarm was also given by telephone to the surrounding towns and along the farmer telephone line and at present several posses are searching the country for the robbers.

One of the robbers is said to be young John Johnson a son of 'Cow Johnson' who lives over near the Dakota line and who is not more than seventeen years of age. The other man is but little older and their daring is nearly beyond belief.

It is also reported that two young men answering their description held up a hardware store at Bainville Monday evening and took only firearms.

As we go to press (Thursday noon) it is thought their escape is impossible and that one of the searching parties will 'round them up this afternoon.

Later:—4:30 p. m. One of the robbers who claims his name is Hansen was brought in by J. M. Leonard, after having been captured by the posse about 1 o'clock after a running fight in which several shots were exchanged. About one half of the money was recovered. The capture took place near Mountjoy's farm about eighteen miles east of here, the robber being shot with a rifle in the right shoulder which fractured his shoulder blade and compelled surrender from loss of blood. Sheriff Duggan is still in pursuit of the Johnson boy and unless he (Johnson) reaches the breaks before dark his capture is certain.

Front page of the Thursday, February 11, 1915 edition of the *Medicine Lake Wave*—the morning of the Farmers' Bank robbery. Note reference to Johnny's father as "Cow Johnson". MONTANA STATE HISTORICAL SOCIETY word without giving proper credit. He also gave Associated Press stringer George Tilton a verbal wallop for announcing that Johnny had been apprehended when he had not been.

Then a newspaper in Antelope, Montana, dragged the sheriff into the debate surrounding Johnson's escape by airing Duggan's gripe that he could not obtain any fast horses to pursue the robbers. Doolin resorted to his editorial page to refute that excuse. He pointed out that some of the fastest nags in the country were chewing oats at the Bowman ranch, less than five minutes' walk from the Medicine Lake hotel when the robbery took place. The Dooley *Sun* joined the clamour now almost drowning out the local coyote population when it blasted the *Wave* for its slovenly comments about the sheriff. The *Sun* suggested that Doolin himself should take the job if he knew so much about it. The *Wave* editor replied grimly that he was thankful he wasn't occupying the sheriff's position in the *minds* of the citizens of Sheridan county. (Duggan, by the way, was not re-elected when his term ran out.)

The verbiage dripping off the pages of the newspapers did not contain the one thing I was looking for—a description of Johnny Johnson. A description, if it had appeared, would have allowed me to compare those released when Albert Johnson was on the run, and might have provided me with solid evidence as to whether the two men were one and the same person. The reason for this oversight on the part of the press was obvious— Johnny was a local boy whom just about everyone in the area knew personally. Still, despite my vested interest, I considered it incompetent journalism that I could find not a single description of Johnson, other than one headline referring to "Little Johnny", in a detailed search of microfilms of Montana and North Dakota newspapers. The newsmen were too busy arguing among themselves to properly attend to such details.

The upshot of the press war was the one thing Johnny Johnson, as a fugitive, would not have wanted. Duggan's loss of face made him vow to stick like glue to Johnson's trail until he tracked down the robber. Duggan mailed circulars throughout the west describing the escapee. This, and the information that the Pinkerton Detective Agency was called in to trace Johnson by the insurer of the bank, gave me cause for optimism in my search. Surely the "Pinks" would possess one of the circulars in their voluminous records in New York City. I wrote to them. They had nothing. Frustrated to the point of yanking out my already thinning hair, I searched and searched for a description of Johnson in the local newspapers and found nary a word, not even to the colour of his hair and eyes.

I would have to withdraw, and plan a new strategy yet again.

John Johnson's escape from the clutches of the law left a void not only for the sheriff but for me in my search. It was relatively easy to trace the bank robbery through newspapers in the area after Rustad's lead. However, regarding Johnson's adventures in Wyoming, Rustad had written nothing other than the fact that John was eventually incarcerated in the Montana state penitentiary after having been arrested on a burglary charge in Wyoming! This certainly did not sound like Johnny's style of operation; but if he had been arrested in Wyoming chances were he would appear somewhere in the records of that state's institutions.

I wrote to the Wyoming penitentiary and they responded that there had never been any John Johnson so incarcerated. Thwarted by that reply, I again took the long route, and began systematically reading through all later issues of Montana newspapers, assuming that they would print any subsequent developments in the career of their local big-time crook. Sure enough, in the Plentywood *Herald* issue of October 5, 1915, I found a news item that said Johnny Johnson had been thrown into the Lincoln County jail in Kemmerer, Wyoming, where he had been sentenced for stealing livestock. I wrote to the jail there, and they reported back that there was no one in their records by that name.

Back to the microfilms. I found yet another article that reported that John had been going under the name of "William Hoffman" when arrested. I wrote to Lincoln County again, and there was no William Hoffman either. In the meantime, I had opened a "second front" by writing to Dolores Munden of the Montana State Penitentiary at Deer Lodge. She reported they had John's records and that his alias in Wyoming was "William Hoffner". So he had lifted more than Louis Haefner's guns from him back in Montana! For the third time I wrote to the jail in Wyoming and—at last—this time they had such a man. Having established this as a certainty, I wrote to the Lincoln County court and obtained the documents concerning Johnson's arrest. From these affidavits I garnered the relevant dates, and then wrote to the Wyoming State Archives for copies of the Kemmerer *Camera* covering the days of his arrest and the court trial two months later. Here is John's story as put together from newspaper reports and records in Wyoming.

Riding hell-bent-for-leather west from the schoolhouse across the river from Bainville, Johnny reached Terry, Montana, sold his outfit, and boarded the train. Somewhere along the line he jumped off and popped up in the town of Rock Springs, Wyoming. He went on to the small community of Green River where he spent $700 of his "hard-earned" funds to buy an outfit. Judging from the gear he purchased, which included a couple of horses, saddle, a six-shooter, rifle, and full riding and pack outfits, it would seem that Johnny was going to head for the hills to hunt and possibly trap. He rode up the Green River where he met another lad of his own age, whom he staked to a horse and guns, and then sent him to Rock Springs to buy another saddle. His erstwhile friend disappeared and Johnson eventually went to Rock Springs to find him. Failing to do so he turned north again, riding up the Green River toward the small community of Big Piney.

It is hard to tell from newspaper accounts about the young man if he was just plain unlucky, dumb, or by nature was attracted to individuals who were often on the wrong side of the law. He bumped into a lad named Dan Creedon and went on a week's wolf hunt with him in the Salt River Mountains. Creedon had been in trouble before he met Johnny, while with Johnny, and would be arrested twice more after he met John.

When they returned from their sojourn in the mountains Creedon apparently slipped off with John's outfit including his horses. Johnny, then, in order to catch up with Creedon, stole a horse from James Black's livery stable in Big Piney, only to be picked up by the law a day or two later near the Birch Creek oil fields south of the town. Here he was surrounded by a posse who successfully captured him and flung him into jail.[1]

Johnson incriminated the elusive Creedon who fled for the desert, where he was shot out of the saddle and caught by the horse's owner, James Black, who had been deputized to bring him in. Creedon was placed in the Kemmerer hospital to recover from a shoulder wound. Two months later in late May of 1915, Johnny pleaded guilty to stealing the horse (which he had released before the posse picked him up). Creedon, in turn, was eventually brought to trial, pleaded not guilty, and was exonerated. This must have been galling to young Johnny who claimed the whole idea was Creedon's in the first place.

Thus, after a series of misfortunes where the sixteen-year-old's new friends either stole from him or incited him to commit a crime, the lad finally ended up in jail. He lied about his age, saying he was nineteen—and here again it would seem he made a bad mistake—admitting his true age, he may have gotten some leniency from the judge. Instead he was given eighteen months in the state penitentiary.

The question arises why Johnson fled to Green River, Wyoming? Of all the places he could have gone, he chose the one known as the home base of the men of the Wild Bunch, particularly Butch Cassidy. Butch had not only lived in Rock Springs, but had made his hideout for a time in Brown's Hole, a refuge located on a tributary of the Green River, about seventy miles south of Rock Springs. Did Johnny go there by design, or had Bert Delker advised him to?

In any case, crime certainly was not paying for Johnny: at sixteen years of age he was in jail, and when his term for horse stealing in Wyoming was up he was shipped to Montana to serve time for the bank robbery. Eventually he was released from Montana State Prison along with his brother, Magnor, in

Criminal Warrant

THE STATE OF WYOMING,
County of Lincoln,

To the Sheriff or Constable of any County, Greeting:

WHEREAS, James Black *has this day complained in writing to me on oath, that* Wm Hoffner Peterson *did on or about the* 16 *day of* March *A. D. 1915., at* Big Piney *in the County and State aforesaid,* Did feloniously steal take and lead away two black horses the property of James Black

and prayed that the said Peterson Wm Hoffner *might be arrested and dealt with according to law. Now, therefore, in the name of the State of Wyoming, you are commanded forthwith to apprehend the said* Peterson *and bring* him *before me to be dealt with according to law.*

Given under my hand this 20 *day of* March 1915.

George Dunford
Justice of the Peace

Criminal Warrant for the arrest of a "Peterson" (aka William Hoffner, aka Johnny Johnson). He had robbed Haefner, and later been assisted by Peterson, so these names were uppermost in his mind. The name "Peterson" tends to back up Frank Slim's recollection that the Mad Trapper used the name "Pete" when Slim met him in the Yukon. WYOMING STATE PENITENTIARY

April 1918. His brother joined the army and John returned home to the farm.

When John and Magnor went to prison in 1915, their father, Andrew, was sixty-seven years old. The burden of shame was heavy enough to bear for the struggling immigrant, but on a more practical note he had lost two strong farm hands. The culminating blow for Andrew and his wife came when their daughter, Helga, disappeared mysteriously, never to be heard from again. Saddled by their misery, the elder Johnsons were losing the farm, with little they could do about it.

John valiantly tried to restore the farm. He built a new barn and planted new acreages of wheat and other crops, but the financial burden was too high and the farm was forfeited. John left home for good. The elder Johnsons sold everything and moved into a nearby shack.

The parallel between the inauspicious beginnings of Johnny and Butch Cassidy establish themselves as a strange historical curiosity, and it is interesting to speculate on whether Johnny was consciously styling his life after Butch and the Wild Bunch, or whether it was merely a coincidence. Both men were raised by parents who were dirt poor; the two came under the influence of older men who were inclined to flout the law (in Butch's case the man was named Mike Cassidy); and each arrived in Rock Springs using an alias. Butch's was "Cassidy", (his real name was Robert Leroy Parker). Johnny, as we saw, callously adopted the name of William Hoffner, the man he had robbed.

Both Johnny and Butch went to the Wyoming State Penitentiary for the same offence, horse stealing, and served about the same amount of time before being released. Also, each had been involved in major crimes before reaching Rock Springs, Johnny having robbed a bank, and Butch a mining payroll in Telluride, Colorado.[2]

In fact, Butch Cassidy and his fellow bandits were by no means the only outlaws whose example was writ large in the life of the Badlands settlers, not just in legend, but in actual person—as I discovered when I travelled to the arid plains that sprawl in the eastern lee of the rugged Rocky Mountains.

The land is much more picturesque than I had been led to believe from perusing black and white photos taken in 1915. Now there are scattered copses of trees as well as the occasional windrow planted to stave off the indomitable winds that often course down from the north. The wheat was cut and the grass short and brown, and yet the rolling prairie cast its spell. The limitless distances, the merging of the sky and the land, and the incredible expanse of it all hypnotized me. It stimulated reflection and I pondered what went on in Johnny's mind when he and his brother set out in mid-winter for Bainville.

Johnny was but sixteen years old at the time, and though he may have rustled a few horses, he was not a hardened veteran of life beyond the law. I wondered what motive propelled him to go forth on that ride. Mortgages were eating away at the family fortune, and he wanted to win Thora, his sweetheart;[3] yet there must have been more, and that may have been the influence of the mystique of the region in which Johnny was raised. This was the upper Missouri River that encompassed the Dakotas, Montana, and Wyoming.

The country was not really opened until after the explorations of Lewis and Clark in 1804. They had been preceeded into the district by missionaries, religious zealots who were something indistinguishable from the traders and uncouth mavericks who would follow them. Large fur companies from Canada, the Hudson's Bay and North West outfits, countered by the Missouri Fur Company and the American Fur Company, had also been there and fought over land and allegiances. With them came adventurers and misfits who were not only to leave an indelible imprint on the pages of history, but on impressionable lads, who like the tumbleweeds, would be blown to this area by the winds of political and economic hardship. Legendary giants such as Hugh Glass, William Sublette, Jed Smith, John Colter, and Mike Fink were characteristic products of a violent existence where to be alive meant to be quick with the knife and gun.

Mike Fink could be counted as one whose image loomed bigger than life. He earned a reputation as one of the toughest brawlers of the Missouri River valley. He fought, gambled, drank, and somehow found time to trap and run keel boats as well. One day at Fort Henry (twenty miles south of Bainville today) in 1823, Mike made a wager that he could shoot a cup of rum off the head of an associate. Being drunk at the time did not help his aim and the shot was low, hitting the man squarely in the forehead and killing him instantly. Two weeks later Fink was murdered in a revenge slaying by a friend of the dead man.

The great days of the fur trade passed. United States Army troops arrived to keep tabs on the Indians, who were becoming increasingly restless as they saw their land overrun and treaty after treaty violated by the whites. Gold and silver rushes in South Dakota, Montana, and elsewhere exacted their toll on Indian lands. The inevitable wars climaxed with the massacre of Custer and 264 soldiers of the Seventh Cavalry in 1876. This brought down the full weight of the United States Army onto the Indians, and "pacification" was generally completed by 1881. These battles, too, had brought forth heroes on both sides, many of whom passed through Fort Buford only a few miles south of Bainville. Cavalrymen, and the Indians Chief Joseph, Crazy Horse, and Sitting Bull were examples of valiant men who fought uncompromisingly in the face of unbeatable odds, and to the death if need be.

The legacy of violence continued, but under different auspices. Even before the Indians were subdued, huge cattle herds were inching their way from the south into the northern tier prairie areas. In 1904 a herd of 7,000 cattle—one of the largest ever assembled up to that time—grazed just west of the Johnson's homestead, and occasionally cowboys would drop in for meals. Johnny would have recalled them with a little envy. They were not bound to a plot of land and could come and go as they pleased. He, too, was a horseman, who could and did break steeds for his father. And he, too, was not without some experience handling cattle.

The cowboys who drove the unpredictable longhorn cattle were just as fickle as nature and as dangerous as the beasts they tended. These men were inured to such trail hazards as Indian attacks, rattlesnakes, lightning bolts, and stampedes which could render a man into a bloody pulp if he was unlucky enough to fall in front of a panic-stricken herd. Toughness and tenacity characterized all their pursuits. Their pay was poor, which led the impatient of them to look for other avenues through horse and cattle rustling, or other more notorious crimes. Eventually the image of the folk hero evolved: the bandit who struck at large corporate structures such as banks and railroads that were often unpopular with the settlers because of their intractability with respect to high-interest loans and impertinent land grabs.

A regular rag-tag conglomerate of bandits raided banks and trains in the upper Missouri River drainage throughout the 1890's and the first years of the new century. John Konrad Johnson was raised in the midst of this legacy, and like spring water dripping from a hillside, it was bound to seep into his mind. Many boys were tempted by the "Jessie James syndrome"; a few succumbed. It would appear that Johnny, while making the trip to Bainville, decided to dance to the beat of a different drum. The ghosts of the past were still too real for him.

Yet, looking back from the vantage point of seventy-five years, it is plain that the Wild West of Johnny's imagination was fading, and would never again live as gloriously in reality as it would in the stories and movies of popular culture. In fact, Johnny represents a rather pathetic figure; all the clichés were wrong. The Bainville robbery took place not under a blazing sun but in the dead of winter. Though this may have exhibited the caginess of Delker's experience—it was a lot harder to raise a posse with prospects of a blue northerner sweeping in to chill the marrow of a deputy's bones—it also added to the bandits' difficulties. Secondly, as already mentioned, telephone and tele- graph lines had appeared to render even the fastest horse use- less. And finally, when Sheriff Duggan did call ahead, most of the posse took off not in galloping splendour, but piled into a snow sled and trotted off to intercept the greenhorn raiders.

The entire episode went against the grain of western lore and only served to underline the old adage that "truth is stranger than fiction". The Eagle River shootout, when it came, was more in the tradition of the west, though it was in the north and instead of horses the men travelled by dog teams, breaking yet another cliché; and in the end, it would be another technology—the airplane—that would be Johnny's nemesis.

Butch Cassidy, Johnny's probable "mentor", was a "successful" working criminal for twenty years, with only one arrest. But for Johnny, only in death would his deeds be legendary.[4]

CHAPTER 11

THE ROAD TO FOLSOM PRISON

AFTER JOHNSON'S WYOMING ADVENTURE and the Montana jail term, I was once more hard put to pick up his trail. But for a change Fortune smiled on my quest. Marlene Eide (of the Williams County Historical Society) introduced me by mail to Mrs. Obert Johnson, one of Johnny's nieces and the daughter of Olga Johnson (Johnny's youngest sister) who had married a local lad named Johnny Weirson. Obviously, the daughter, in turn, had married another Johnson. I talked with Mrs. Johnson on the phone and she told me her daughter, Sharon, had been investigating the case and had received a letter from a Montana prison that said John had not only been there and in Wyoming jails, but also had served time in San Quentin in California.

I called Sharon, whose married name is also Johnson(!), and she said she would forward a copy of her note from the San Quentin authorities about John's imprisonment there. She gave me a little more information about the family including Magnor, who had served in the First World War in the 88th Infantry Division, had been wounded, and had received the Purple Heart medal. After the war he had married and settled in Benson, Minnesota. Later, he was successful in the fuel distribution business. Sharon said Johnny's sister, Helga, never was found, and that her (Sharon's) grandmother, Olga, died of tuberculosis in the thirties.

Sharon once journeyed to Regina, Saskatchewan, where she visited the Royal Canadian Mounted Police Museum to apprise them of the facts concerning her great-uncle, but they were not of much help. And, since she possessed no photos of John, nor a description of him, there was little the Mounties could do to help establish that Albert was Johnny.

When I received the note from Sharon concerning California, I saw that I was stumped once more. There was no mention of the crime or where it was committed. I wrote the Vacaville Discharge Center of the prison, and they told me all records had been destroyed. I thought about that for half a year, and decided to take one last fling with the office of the Attorney General of the state. I had learned by now to mention not only John's real name, but also his latest alias: at the time of his arrest in California he was going under the name Charles W. Johnson.

To my surprise, the Attorney General's office came back with a lead. They referred me to the state archives. I never thought that *prison* records might be in a state archives, but I suppose after fifty-five years everything becomes an artifact. A copy of Johnson's physical examination was sent to me, and on it was the place of his arrest: Susanville, California.[1] The crime had again been grand larceny, and the offence the same as Wyoming. Johnny had repeated his previous escapade and stolen a horse. I guess once a guy gets into a rut he just can't get out of it.

At this point I went into high gear. I wrote to the Lassen County Court House for records of John's trial, to the local county jail, and to the state archives to obtain photocopies of newspapers covering his arrest and trial. Bruce Dyer of the County Records department very considerately copied the court records from which I obtained names of the jurors and other people involved in the case.

One way to find leads, even when a case has been in limbo for fifty years, is to look for people who had been involved, especially whose names are a bit unusual, and to phone them. (It's just easier to find them in a directory!) I did this in respect to Goddard Long, whose father was one of the men who arrested Johnson near Susanville, and who was mentioned in the preliminary hearing as having accompanied the elder Long when they discovered his dad's horse had been stolen. Telephone Information gave me the number of a Goddard Long in Susanville, and I

'ING CT LET

·tion Com-ntract for ; to Begin)ays.

board of city bt the contract street was let ·tion company rren company to bid on the

.e in as much pe(paving bid, on the basis of ni. to be done, out $3000 over

ation received country street about ten per d a year ago tees are to be persistency in criticism and he basis of the nville's paving less than the costing other

dnesday night was instructed ns for the im- d Weatherlow

he contract the

HORSE THIEF ARRESTED IN BIG VALLEY

Sunday evening two saddle horses belonging to the Sierra Packing Company, were stolen from the Woods and Geiger slaughter house. Sheriff Church got on the job right away and Wednesday he arrested a man giving the name of Chas. W. Johnson, whom the sheriff has every reason to believe is one of the men who took the saddle horses.

Two men had been seen hanging around the slaughter house just previous to the theft of the horses. The sheriff started out on the trail Monday morning with Henry Baughman, who has some reputation as a tracker. They trailed the stolen horses out through eastern Lassen county and found where one of the horses had broken loose and returned to Willow Creek near Merrillville. This left one man on foot and the sheriff and Baughman followed the tracks of the other horse out through the Madeline country. They camped out one night and Wednesday they found their man in Big Valley. He had turned the horse loose, evidently finding out that he was being followed. The saddle was found under a tree and the horse at the Anderson place near Hayden Hill. Johnson was found in a cabin and taken into custody.

The horses were not hurt any by their experience, and as both are valuable animals the packing company is glad to have them back. Sheriff Church expects to get the other man right away, and he is to be commended on the energy and activity he displayed in the matter.

o

GOOD] HIGI

**Surveyors Bouleva for Joh Other **

State highw ty is movin of surveyors will begin wo end of the Seitz inform party will co a cook, and about twenty

The contr. had a hes b the Highwa double work tire in the

The Highw. received adve land over t Corral about ·lle.

Work on th and Westwoo satisfactorily is in charge Talley is sup

The contra was right abo let. This s length and out through close proxim probably jus account of necessarily called person-to-person. A woman answered the phone and at first seemed somewhat reluctant to talk. I realized that her husband may have passed away many years ago and she would be perplexed by a stranger who wanted to discuss a sixty-year-old rustling case. We talked further and I explained my object in the case and Mrs. Long graciously agreed to help me out, particularly in finding old photos of the area, and possibly of some of the principals involved, including her late husband. She also looked up the case for me in the local library and its newspaper files. From this I reconstructed the story of Johnson's arrest as far as I could.

Johnny apparently went west hoping to restore his fortunes in some way. He reached the Sierras of California and presumably worked at a number of jobs in logging and mining camps before he ran afoul of the law, and again his culpability in the crime was at least partly in question. Two horses were stolen from the Sierra Packing Company located in Susanville, on the night of May 22, 1921. Thomas H. Long, one of the co-owners of the packing company looked over the scene of the theft and noticed two different sets of footprints, suggesting there were two rustlers involved. He judged the guilty parties might be tracked down because of the distinguishing characteristics in one of the thieves' shoe soles: one man's shoes had hobnails, though the other's did not. He called in Sheriff J. S. Church, who in turn sought the services of Isaac Henry Baughman, known throughout the Sierras as an expert tracker. The two men and Long set out in a car with their horses tethered behind, and slowly followed the tracks of the stolen horses. One of them was a bay gelding that was "barefoot", as Baughman later put it in court. The other horse had two shoes. The combination of these distinctive prints together on the horses and their thieves made pursuit of them simpler. However the road over which the thieves had fled received a fair amount of traffic consisting of horsemen, wagons and cars.

May 27, 1921 issue of the *Lassen Advocate* reporting Johnson's arrest (under the alias "Charles Johnson") for rustling—his fourth (known) act of robbery to this date. CALIFORNIA STATE LIBRARY

The three men followed the hoofprints from the Sierra Packing Company's corral to a nearby wagon road. From there the thieves had ridden their horses across the top of a hill to return again to the road. Part-way across the hill the rustlers had dismounted. Baughman picked up the hobnailed and smooth shoe prints. Back on the road again, the three followers observed that the thieves had remounted.

Baughman and the others lost the tracks at this point and did not pick them up again until that night using a spotlight on the car. The tracks they found were of the bay gelding, the shoeless horse. Prints of the other horse and rider had disappeared. They followed the gelding's trail for three or four miles north until the track vanished from the road. As it was now after midnight, the three men went another mile and then camped for the night. Figuring the thieves might have doubled back, the next morning, using their horses, the trackers returned the way they had come, and in so doing passed a man walking north on foot, in hobnail boots. So they were right: the man had circled round, come back to the road *behind* them, and was heading north again.

Baughman observed the footprints and noted that the shoes had some of the hobnails missing so that the wearer left the same print that one of their thieves had left since leaving the Sierra Packing Company's corral. Also, from "what little description" they had from different parties, Baughman, Church, and Long figured the man they had passed on the road was the same one who had stolen the gelding. However, not wanting to tip him off yet, they continued along the road in the opposite direction to him, and shortly thereafter discovered the man's camp a short distance off the road. Diligently examining the campsite, they found the bay's shoeless hoofprints and Long's saddle hidden behind a tree, thus linking the hobnail prints with those of the stolen horse. That was all Sheriff Church needed for evidence to arrest the thief.

Baughman deduced what had happened. On hearing the approach of the car the night before, the culprit had ridden off among the junipers and waited until the vehicle had gone by. He had remained there until early morning, taken the saddle off the horse, and released it. With the damning evidence now in hand, Baughman traced the hobnailed bootprints back to the road and along it to the point where he, Church, and Long had passed the suspect earlier that day. The three followed his trail until the hobnails disappeared into a rock canyon near their car. Baughman speculated that their quarry had doubled back again, but sensing that the thief had a particular destination in mind farther up the road, suggested that they continue on north. The small posse travelled on a way and was told by several people in the vicinity that the stagecoach had picked up the fellow they were probably looking for and given him a ride to the small town of Bieber. Baughman and the others sped there, but found that the stage driver had not picked up anyone. So they backtracked until they found the hobnailed tracks yet again. The telltale marks followed the road for three hundred yards where they led to some shacks in a flat on an old home-stead about a quarter of a mile or so away. The three men surrounded the only occupied cabin and with guns drawn, called out the suspect and Sheriff Church arrested him.

The alleged thief claimed his name was Charles W. Johnson,[2] and steadfastly denied any part in the crime. He was taken to Susanville, and since theft of livestock in California and in most of the western states was classified as grand larceny, he was held for trial. If he had any identification papers, he had either hidden them or thrown them away.

Johnny was back in trouble again. Two trials resulted in hung juries, but on the third John was convicted of stealing one horse, sentenced, and shipped off to San Quentin. After a month there, he was sent to Folsom Prison where he served a year. At the end of this time the prison board met and sentenced him to seven and a half more years. However, two months later, December 22, 1922, he was paroled, probably because it was Christmas and Johnson's behaviour had been acceptable.

In looking at this arrest, there was not much to go on in establishing Johnny Johnson as Albert, other than two habits. One was Johnny's inclination to stubbornly remain in the area of the crime rather than to immediately flee the country without looking back. Why he did not head for the high country imme-

A view of Folsom Prison where Johnny Johnson spent a year for horse thievery. CALIFORNIA STATE LIBRARY

diately after stealing the horse is a mystery, and his decision to return to the road and to his cabin after he released the horse is another act that seems completely illogical. As previously observed, Albert Johnson's inclinations were much the same after he shot King and Millen. Rather than make a beeline for a distant place, he hung around the Rat River, seemingly satisfied that he could elude his pursuers this way. Of course, the conditions at forty and fifty below zero were different from those in balmy California, but the peculiarly inappropriate behaviour for a criminal was still there.

Tending to confirm this theory are a psychiatrist's remarks concerning Albert Johnson's failure to run after shooting King at his Rat River cabin. (When the posse came back a week later he was still there.) The psychiatrist said, "Some people cannot think accurately and don't look ahead to the consequences of their acts. Johnson had a problem in that he wanted to be left strictly alone and this interfered with his logical and realistic thinking on the matter. He simply felt that shooting at those men, and hitting one of them, would cause them to go away and leave him alone."[3]

There was another likeness between the two Johnsons: the lack of identification papers or anything giving a clue to either man's past. Johnny gave an alias when he was picked up. If he really was innocent, why was he going under an assumed name? He had served time and had been released from jail. Of course, he may have figured his true name and previous record might be held against him, even if he was innocent this time. But the contrary indications are stronger. The alias may have been intended to hide the fact that he had violated parole. And the lack of papers seems to indicate he had been up to even more mischief for which he had not been caught, and for which he had prepared to hide his identity.

One other similarity was the strategy Johnny used when he was being followed by tracker Baughman: his habit of doubling back. He did this three different times while on the road to Bieber. Albert Johnson likewise followed the same tactic, but was foiled several times when he turned back on his trail too early and found that he was still in front of his pursuers rather than behind them.

The most important thing to look for in establishing the unity of Albert Johnson and John Johnson is their physical descriptions. Before I delve into John Johnson's prison records I should point out that nowhere in newspaper accounts concerning the four known transgressions of the law in which Johnny was involved south of the border was there anything describing him in written form. The nearest thing to that was a headline in a Montana newspaper about "little" Johnny Johnson escaping the sheriff's posse. This omission was the major loophole in the theory; plugging it would now become my primary preoccupation in cementing the identification of the two Johnsons as the same.

CHAPTER 12

FINGERPRINTS—LET THE SLEEPING DOG LIE

IT HAD BECOME CRUCIAL to my search that I obtain copies of Johnny's prison records and the information therein to reinforce the supposition that John Johnson and Albert Johnson were one and the same. If any major physical characteristic were different—colour of hair or eyes, for example—the cross-referencing would fall apart. If I could obtain photos of Johnny that would be so much the better.

Most of the county jails of that era have not retained records of their inmates. However, I was fortunate enough to obtain copies of John's records from the Lincoln County jail in Kemmerer, Wyoming, which provided me with a profile of John at the age of sixteen years eleven months. On giving information to the authorities there, he had fibbed about his age, stating that he was nineteen. His weight was listed as 144 pounds and his height read five feet eight and three-quarter inches. Johnny's complexion was described as "light florid", reddish in hue, as is that of many Scandinavians. His hair was "light chestnut", the beard was light. His eyes were blue and he gave as his occupation a ranch hand. Johnny told the examining physician he was of German-American descent, which he wasn't, and that he was from California, also a lie. As previously mentioned, John told the jailers and the court that his name was William Hoffner, and so that was the name under which he was incarcerated.

Under "marks and scars" the following items were in Johnson's prison file: "spot scar left elbow joint, large wart on palm of left hand, large brown birthmark on median link center of

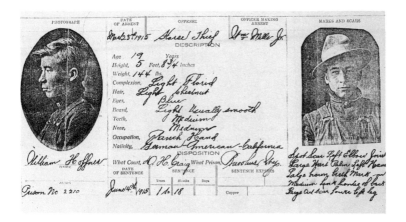

Johnny Johnson in Lincoln County Jail, Kemmerer, Wyoming, under the alias "William Hoffner". Copies of these photos were sent to trappers John Robert, Tom Smith, Arthur John, and Paul Nieman for identification, with positive results. LINCOLN COUNTY JAIL

back, and a large cut scar on the lower left leg."

Johnny was moved from the Lincoln County jail to the penitentiary at Rawlins where the usual data about him was recorded, including his fingerprints, the classification of which was listed as right hand 11R I0 20 and left, 4-00 17.[1] After Johnny completed his Wyoming jail term he was transferred to the Sheridan County jail in Montana and held for trial for the bank robbery. He pleaded guilty and in September, 1916, was sentenced to "from three to ten years at hard labor" in Montana State Prison, thereby joining his half-brother in Deer Lodge. Here records showed that he again lied about his age, giving it as twenty-two when he was actually eighteen.

A synopsis of his physical exam at Deer Lodge also mentions the birthmark in the centre of his lower back, and additional information not found in Wyoming records. Johnny's teeth were classified as "poor". His chin was described as "round".

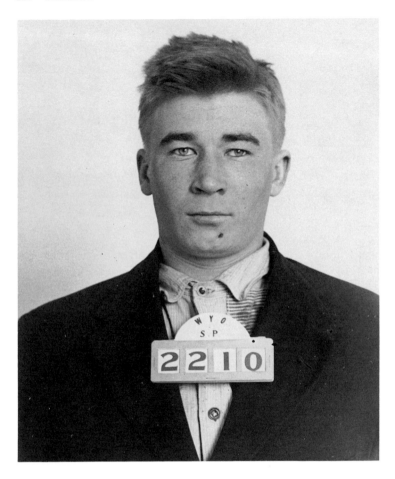

Mug shot of Johnny as he entered Wyoming State Penitentiary at seventeen years of age. Notice how the left eye is slightly askew.
WYOMING STATE ARCHIVES

Bertillon measurements of John's head, trunk, left foot, left middle finger, left little finger, left forearm, and right ear were given, but since Dr. Urquhart made no such measurements (other than the foot) in examining Albert Johnson, they are not listed here.[2] He was described as having a cataract on his left eye, a one-inch scar on his right kneecap, and a small mole below the right nipple on his chest. His fingerprints were also taken: right hand—11R I0 19; left hand—4-00 17.

On August 13, 1921, John entered San Quentin under the alias Charles W. Johnson. He gave his age as twenty-eight when it was actually twenty-three. He had apparently begun to think about Canada as that is where he told authorities he was born. He told them he was a machinist by trade, which was probably true as he may have learned the occupation in Deer Lodge.

John's height had increased to five feet nine and one-quarter inches and his weight to 169 pounds. His build was described as "muscular", where before it was "medium". Bertillon measurements and profile were about the same as those in Montana. The birthmark on his back was again mentioned. It was noted that his nose was "deep rooted" (i.e., flaring nostrils), and his forehead was described as "receding". He had two scars on the right side of his left palm indicating the wart that was on this hand in Wyoming had now been removed. His prints read: right hand—11R I0 19, left—4-00 17.

Let's compare the material from the three penitentiaries, and Dr. Urquhart's description of Albert Johnson. Albert's height was estimated to be from five feet nine to five feet nine and one-half inches. Albert's estimated weight was 145 to 150 pounds. Since he was terribly emaciated it would appear the weight was solely a guess, but it was within the range of Johnny's since he had probably lost twenty to thirty pounds during the chase.

Albert was described as having light brown hair beginning to recede at the forehead, and he parted it on the left side. John's hair was "light chestnut", also parted on the left side. His San Quentin examination revealed a receding hairline (though he was only twenty-three years old at the time). Albert's hair growth on his face, chin, and upper lip was light brown like John's.

The trapper's eyes were described as pale blue. Johnny's were blue. Albert's nose was snubbed with the ridge slightly convex. There was no reference to John's being "snubbed" though it is

Mug shot of Johnny from San Quentin. Despite his being a little older, similarities are obvious: the very faint cleft in the chin, the slightly protruding lower lip, and the single wrinkle under the eye.
CALIFORNIA STATE LIBRARY

obvious from photographs that it was turned up at the tip and the ridge was also convex.

Albert's cheekbones were "moderately prominent", a feature also evident in John Johnson's photo. Albert's ears were "low set" and close to the head and lobed, these traits evident also in John's photo. In the death photo, Albert's left ear is obviously striated by frostbite and his right seems to be dehydrated with the lobe insignificant—which appears to directly contradict Urquhart's own statement that the ears were heavily lobed.

Dr. Urquhart's examination of Albert revealed a "small wart or mole two inches to the left of the spine in the mid lumbar region". John's records showed a brown birthmark in the centre or "median" link of his back.

Urquhart stated there were no "operation scars or evidence of old fractures" on the trapper's corpse. Urquhart did not mention a vaccination or circumcision scar, which would of course have been an "operation" scar and was commonly recorded in physical examinations.

Johnny Johnson's records reported no operation scars or evidence of old fractures, though he had several scars of a "non-operational" nature. Nowhere in the three prisons was it noted that John had a vaccination scar or a circumcision scar.

Urquhart estimated Albert Johnson's age to have been between thirty-five and forty years. Johnny, if he were Albert, would have been thirty-three years and seven months old at the time of his death.

Albert Johnson's teeth were described as having numerous fillings, crowns, extractions and bridges, indicating they had once been in poor condition.

Similarly, Johnny's teeth were described as poor in his prison records. No complete dental records were still in existence, other than the "poor" reference.

Death photographs of Albert Johnson and photos obtained of John Johnson from various penitentiaries were mailed to Dr. J. V. Clark of Mayo, Yukon Territory. Clark had three decades of experience with frostbite cases in a town that has recorded the second lowest temperature in North America (81° below zero F.). He patiently compared the photos and wrote:

> There is nothing in these photographs to indicate they [Albert and John] are not the same person. The malar bones and supraorbital ridges above the eyes are similar. The right ears are similar; so are the eyelids. Other evidence such as the disappearance of John Johnson (William Hoffner, Charles W. Johnson) from history when Albert Johnson died, etc., along with these photographs, would be pretty solid evidence that they are one and the same person.

I also submitted the photos to A. V. Iannarelli of Fremont, California, one of the foremost experts on ear identification and author of *System of Ear Identification* (Foundation Press of Brooklyn, New York, 1968). He found marked similarities between the right ears of the two subjects, pointing out there were exact comparisons in the start of the helix rim (where the ear curls out from the skull in an upward sweep) and the minute creases in the upper portion of the same rim, and general likenesses in the triangularity of the ear, its normal size, and its closeness to the head. However, he declined to submit a conclusion on his identity.

On my "mental chalkboard" where I kept track of evidence corroborated by photos, physical description and general demeanour (modus operandi), the checkmarks indicating that Johnny and Albert were one and the same person were slowly beginning to add up.

Before I go further, I should add the fact that, in his report on John Johnson, Wallace Rustad had stated that a death photo of Albert Johnson had been shown to John's mother, Petra, when she was in the Ambrose senior citizens' home in North Dakota, in about 1937. Reluctantly and with much grief she reportedly said the man in the photo was her son. Unfortunately, Rustad did not "footnote" this observation to say who showed the photo to Petra or where the photo had come from. Even if he had provided the details, it still did not absolutely *prove* John and Albert were one and the same person. But it certainly added weight to the information piling up on the "plus" side.

I had come now to the watershed—the last hurdle in my search for evidence that would undeniably link the two Johnsons. The only recourse for me was to obtain Albert's fingerprints, which the RCMP claimed they no longer possessed. Since Albert was buried in permafrost his skin would likely be preserved enough to "lift" the prints after disinterring his body. As every police manual states: Fingerprints constitute the only absolutely certain means of identification ever discovered.[3] Nevertheless I was reluctant to initiate this step, considering the amount of red tape I'd have to unravel to receive approval for such a project. I weighed the pros and cons. I was wallowing in endless volumes of information culled from fifteen years of research, all of it done in my spare time, unpaid, driven only by the "need to know". Should I forgo this last, most scientific proof, or should I go on? I decided on the latter. The only thing I had to lose fighting the red tape was my hair.

If the reader gets nothing else out of this book he or she will at least learn the procedures for digging up a body in Canada's Northwest Territories. Granted, the information might not be of much practical use but, if employed as a conversation opener, one could be assured of being one of the few persons knowledgeable on the subject.

In 1981 I visited the office of the Department of Vital Statistics in the Yukon in Whitehorse, and asked the clerk how I would go about exhuming a body. She gave me a rather stern look at first, and then shrugged—clerks are used to having tourists plodding into that office with insane questions—and told me to write to the equivalent office in Yellowknife, capital of the N.W.T. Instead of writing I called, and they sent me a copy of the regulations covering the subject. The process was not as complicated as I thought it would be.

The principal items to be acquired were the written consent

of the cemetery owner and the medical officer in charge of the area in which the cemetery was found. After obtaining such permission I was to make application to the Registrar General of the Territory and state the location of the body, purpose of the disinterment, and the place where the body was to be reburied. The usual fees were to be attached. Then the Registrar General would either grant permission or turn it down.

I wrote to the Reverend Geoffrey Dixon of All Saints Church in Aklavik, in whose jurisdiction the cemetery lay. In my letter I enclosed the pertinent information I had acquired concerning Albert and Johnny Johnson. I added that anxiety over the mystery weighed heavily on the shoulders of John's relatives over the years. Obsessed as I was personally with firmly identifying the Mad Trapper, this next step was a particularly sobering reminder that the relatives of men shot by Johnson were equally interested in seeing the case solved. I was thinking particularly of the family of Edgar Millen who had died in the prime of his life.

Exhuming Albert's body and taking his fingerprints would serve to settle once and for all whether Johnny was Albert. Along with my letter I enclosed copies of my correspondence with the Mounties concerning Albert's burial in the cemetery on March 9, 1932, and the coroner's inquest of February 18, 1932.

Reverend Dixon promptly responded that he had passed the letter along to the Bishop of the Arctic, John Sperry. In a short time I had my answer. As far as the bishop was concerned he had no objections to the exhumation, but he pointed out that permission to proceed was primarily a concern of the Northwest Territories government. Unknown to me at the time, but in good faith, Reverend Dixon approached the Aklavik hamlet council and asked if they would permit the exhumation of Johnson. Later, in a letter of January 12, 1982, he informed me that the council was against it. In the meantime I enclosed the bishop's letter with the other material, including a copy of Johnny Johnson's prints, and sent the package to the Regional Director of Health and Welfare, Dr. J. D. Martin, in Yellowknife. Martin wrote that there were no objections to the exhumation process in his department, but that he had forwarded all my material to the Chief Coroner of the Northwest Territories, Raymond James, the man with the final say in such matters.

A month went by before I received a reply from the chief coroner. The response that came, however, opened new horizons on the case. It was as if the lid had blown off and failed to come down.

James, a retired member of the Royal Canadian Mounted Police, who for a number of years served in Dawson City as the detachment commander there, turned down my request, but not without considerable research. He had written to the Criminal Investigation Branch of the RCMP in Ottawa and they sent their file on the case to the coroner. This file is not in the historical section where most information is garnered by writers like me, but is on microfilm in RCMP archives. James patiently waded through the entire file looking for material on Johnny Johnson. Ultimately he came up with only two references to him and he wrote to me about both. One concerned brothers, Martin and Oscar Haug, who reported having known Johnny Johnson; their farm in North Dakota was four miles from his father's. Having read a story about Albert Johnson and seen an accompanying photo of him in a "detective magazine" they were reasonably sure that Johnny and Albert were one and the same. On a fishing trip in Canada in 1944 the brothers had visited the Mountie museum and while looking at a display dealing with the Mad Trapper case had remarked that they knew Johnson. The Haugs were subsequently questioned by a member of the Force. They told him that Petra Johnson, mother of Johan Konrad, was also sure it was her son after she saw the pictures and the article was read to her. (I think that this last information, however, would at best require some qualification: she could not read, write, or speak English.)

Even so, this served to support Rustad's undocumented comment to the same effect. I could have congratulated myself if it had not been for the first part of James' letter which stated that the opposite was irrefutably true. I quote:

Northwest
        Territories Justice and Public Services

                                                    January 20, 1982.

Mr. Dick North,
P.O. Box 5118,
WHITHORSE, Yukon.
Y1A 4S3.

Dear Mr. North:

Your letters and all attachments dated October 5th 1981
and December 7th 1981 to Dr. J. D. Martin, Chief Medical
Officer have been forwarded to me for consideration for
exhumation of the remains of Albert Johnson under Section
15(4) of the Coroner's Ordinance.

The only purpose for consideration in this matter appears
to be an attempt to identify the deceased Albert Johnson
as actually being one Johan Konsad Jonsen, born in Norway
July 13th 1898. In pursuit of this endeavour you enclosed
copies of fingerprints of Johan Jonsen @ John Johnson.

Your enquiry prompted me to have the complete R.C.M.Police
file forwarded to Yellowknife from Ottawa. The complete
file has now been reviewed and two pieces of evidence were
found which refute your theory that Albert Johnson was in
fact John Johnson.

Unfortunately the fingerprints taken from Albert Johnson
after his death were held on file for several years but
have since been disposed of. However, a memo dated March
9th 1937 from the Director of Criminal Intelligence indicates
that Albert Johnson's fingerprints show that the pattern
of his left forefinger is a radial loop and his left middle
finger is an ulnar loop. John Johnson's fingerprints as
supplied by you were checked by the R.C.M.Police Identification Section and it was found that the left forefinger
is a double loop and the left middle finger is a whorl
pattern. This eliminates John Johnson as being Albert
Johnson.
                                            .../2

- 2 -

It was also found that two brothers, Martin and Oscar Haug, who lived 13 miles south of Grenora, N.D. reported knowing Johan Konrad Johnsen, whose farm was 4 miles away. Having read the story of Albert Johnson and seeing accompanying pictures of him, they were reasonably sure they were the same person. While in Canada on a fishing trip in 1944, these brothers visited the R.C.M.Police Museum in Regina where they made the comment that they knew Johnson, while looking at the display dealing with the "Mad Trapper" case. They were subsequently questioned by a member of the R.C.M.Police. At that time they said that Petra Johnsen, mother of Johan Konrad, was also sure it was her son after she saw the pictures and read the article about the Albert Johnson case. As a result, a comparison of fingerprints was made and Johan Konrad Johnsen was eliminated as being one and the same person as "Albert Johnson". Mrs. Petra Johnsen was advised of this.

Many letters were received by the R.C.M.Police following release of the Albert Johnson story from people claiming knowledge of the identity of the dead man. All of these were carefully eliminated by identifying marks, physical characteristics or fingerprints. The real identity of Albert Johnson remains a mystery.

The above indicates to me that the possibility of Albert Johnson being Johan Konrad Jonsen has already been examined and eliminated and that the description of Albert Johnson's fingerprints does not compare with those of Johan Konrad Jonsen. I therefore cannot justify the making of an order under the Coroner's Ordinance to exhume these remains.

                              Yours sincerely,

                         (signed) R. L. James,
                                  Chief Coroner.

c.c. C. Praamsa
      Health & Welfare, Canada.

Letter from R. L. James, Chief Coroner, Northwest Territories, informing author of the loss of part of Johnson file. RCMP ARCHIVES

Unfortunately the fingerprints taken from Albert Johnson after his death . . . have since been disposed of. However, a memo dated March 9th, 1937, . . . indicates that Albert Johnson's fingerprints show that the pattern of his left forefinger is a radial loop and his left middle finger is an ulnar loop.

John Johnson's fingerprints as supplied by you were checked by the RCMP Identification Section and it was found that the left forefinger is a double loop and the left middle finger is a whorl pattern. This eliminates John Johnson as being Albert Johnson. . . .

It would seem, then, that this was the end of the road. I could cross John off my list of leads and continue my search elsewhere. Yet even when the door seemed slammed shut, something made me suspect that possibly I was not yet through with Johnny Johnson. Now at least I had the patterns of two of Albert's fingerprints to work with. I could thank James for this. The fact that he had mentioned the Haugs' observations also opened another window. I traced Oscar Haug to Silverton, Oregon, and wrote to him about his recognition of Johnny, and waited for an answer.

In the meantime I pondered the 1937 memo to which Dr. James' letter referred. Obviously it had not been written without a reason. There must have been some incident that had prompted it in the first place. I wrote to James again and asked him if he would enlighten me on this point. He complied with my request. The memo had originated because of an inquiry written to the director by one Julian Folvag, who, judging from the tone of the memo, had been told that John and Albert were one and the same. The director had passed the query to W. W. Watson, the officer in charge of Identification Services. He in his turn had written, "apparently Mr. Julian Folvag has received the wrong information from [the warden of] Montana State Prison as the finger print *classification* given by the Warden of the State Prison distinctly shows two whorl patterns—one in the left index finger and one in the left middle finger . . ." (my italics).

Watson went on to say that if the classification by the prison chief was correct, it would be impossible for the two men to be identical. He said that the warden furnished only the classification, not the actual prints. The head jailer also sent along a description and photograph of John Johnson. Watson said he would seek to obtain John's actual prints and he would advise the director as to the results of this. That was the extent of the note and the extent of the RCMP file on the subject.

As if tracking the loner himself, I plodded back, from one footprint to the one behind it. I now knew the reason for the memo, but it gave rise to another question: why had Folvag written to Montana State Prison in 1937?

Let me fill in the background as I pieced it together. According to the Williams County history, Folvag's father, Henry, and mother, Mary, had settled near the Johnson homestead in 1907. In 1914, the elder Folvag opened a coal mine on Cottonwood Creek less than a mile from the Johnsons' farm and operated it for twenty-five years. Julian was born in 1908. He was ten when Johnny returned to Climax after his stint in Montana State Penitentiary in 1918. Julian and a brother took over the operation of the Folvag mine in 1932. Thus, when he wrote the letter to the Mounties in 1937 Julian was well versed in the subject of Johnny Johnson. The reason he had written the letter was due to the decline of the Johnson family. By this time Johnny's mother was elderly and in a senior citizens' home. His father had died in the twenties; his sister Helga had disappeared; his sister Signe had died in childbirth; his sister Olga died of tuberculosis; and his half-brother Magnor, having served time in Montana State Prison for the bank robbery, was somewhere in Minnesota successfully rehabilitating himself, and not eager to dig into the past. Not even Olga's widower, Johnny Weirson, was around. For a time he was away, leaving his two daughters, Angie and Vernie, to be raised by Weirson's father and mother. I guessed that the letter had been written by the long-time neighbour at the request of Johnny's mother, Petra, when the detective-magazine story came out, and someone noticed the similarity between the pictures in the magazine and the young Johnny.

Oscar Haug finally wrote to me and reiterated the statement he had made to the Mounties in 1944. I quote:

"The folks had a detective book with a perfect picture of John, and everybody that seen that picture said it was Johnny." The fact that John had disappeared into Canada in 1923[4] backed up their assumption that John and Albert were one and the same.

I continued backtracking. The detective magazine photo Folvag referred to was the same one that had been spotted by Ed Asp and George Adsit in Dease Lake, British Columbia. They had been the first witnesses to confirm way back in 1937, the report from Ross River, Yukon Territory, that the dead man was the same man that had been known as Arthur Nelson when he trapped near Dease Lake. In other words, the photograph of the dead trapper that, sixty years later, Haug still affirmed was a photo of *Johnny* Johnson was also a photo of the same man that had told Buttle he was from North Dakota—the one clue that had put me on the trail so long ago.

Folvag's letter on behalf of the aged Mrs. Johnson was a fortuitous event that had triggered the comparison of two of Albert's fingerprints with two of John's prints. If Folvag had not written, this reference would not have been available.

I should point out that Montana State Prison had sent me microfilm copies of the correspondence between them and Inspector Watson of the RCMP in 1932 and 1937. This exchange of letters was not in the RCMP files, as Coroner James had come up with only two references to John Johnson; in fact, there were no fewer than nine letters.

In the correspondence begun in June, 1932, Watson had requested Johnny's fingerprints. What led to that RCMP query is not known, but the information could have come from just about anyone who had known Johnny. Montana State Prison, as we have noted in Watson's memo, did not send him the prints themselves, but they did send him the fingerprints' classification. One look was all Watson needed to see that the two classifications were so far apart they could never be related. He said as much in writing back to the Montana warden.

Seemingly, this closed the issue. However, five years later when Folvag sent in his query, there was a new warden at the penitentiary. Folvag in his letter of February 1, 1937, sought John's fingerprint classification and asked if John and Albert were the same. In replying to Folvag, the new warden said,

"They [RCMP] replied that Albert Johnson and John Johnson were without a doubt the same party." What Watson actually had written was "there is no doubt that John Johnson is not identical with Albert Johnson." Obviously, the new warden or his secretary had not read past the words "no doubt".

This inspired Folvag to then write directly to the Mounties giving rise to the C.I.B. director's note to which Watson had replied on March 9 (the fifth year to the day after Albert's burial at Aklavik). Watson, as he had promised, wrote to Montana State Prison on March 10 asking the warden to send him the actual fingerprints. He also pointed out the error Montana had made in the prison's letter to Folvag.

The warden wrote back to Watson a week later and apologized for the mistake. This time he also included Johnny Johnson's fingerprints. He also wrote to Folvag to explain the error. (By now poor Folvag probably wondered which end was up!)

On March 20, 1937, after reviewing the actual prints, Watson wrote to the Montana State Penitentiary and again reiterated that John and Albert were not the same.

This might have closed the issue for me too. But twenty years on the trail had made something of a detective out of me, against all odds. As I said earlier, James' inclusion of a description of Albert Johnson's fingerprints opened a new vista on the case, and I'll explain how. But first, a layman's course in fingerprint examination is necessary. Ridges on the skin of the fingers form patterns; and all fingerprint patterns can be grouped into three main categories: loops, whorls, and arches. Whorls are spiral or

Genoira N. Dakota
Feb 1st 1931

Dear Sirs:

Can you give me any
information of a John
Johnson who served time
in The Deer Lodge Institution
the years of 1919 To 1931 for a
Bank Robbery Committed at
Medicine Lake Montana
in the month of Feb. 1916
Have you his finger print Clasified
on file or a photograph of of him
That Could Be obtained from you
as an unidentified Criminal was
Killed a few years ago which
was albert Johnson But its Believed
the name albert was an alias
and it may be the John Johnson
I am asking information of as
age Hight weight Color of hair ect
Corresponds But John. he has not

Been seen By his folk since
1923 it Could Be some one else
and would Be very pleased
to get his finger print
Classifications as he Could
Maybe Be indentified that way
I am enclosing a self addressed
stamped envelope hoping
you Can give Me some
information of this man.
        Sincerely yours.
    Wm. Julian Folvag
            Glenora
                N. Dak.

Letter written by Julian Folvag on behalf of Johnny's dying mother to the Montana State Prison. The prison officials then wrote to the RCMP, which was the letter that prompted the only remaining memo in the RCMP file. MONTANA STATE PRISON

```
                                        Grenora N.Dakota
                                        Feb 1st 1937

Dear Sirs:

        Can you give me any information of a John Johnson
who served time in The Deer Lodge Instution the years
of 1919 to 1921 for a Bank Robbery commited at Medicine
Lake Montana in the Month of Feb. 1916 Have you his
finger print classification on file or a photograph of
of him that could Be obtained from you as an unidentified
Criminal was Killed a few years ago which was Albert Johnson
But its Beliefed the Nname albert was an alias and it may
be the John Johnson I am asking information of as age
Height weight color of hair ect. Corresponds But John he has
not Been seen By his folk since 1923 it Could Be some one
else and would Be Very pleased to get his finger print
classifications as he could maybe Be identified that way
I am enclosing a self addressed stamped envelope hoping
you can give Me some information of this man.

                                        Sincerely yours

                                Mr. Julian Folvag

                                        Grenora

                                        N. Dak.
```

circular patterns, loops are lines that turn back, like the closed end of a bobby pin, while arches enter from one side of the pattern and leave at the other side with a slight rise in the middle. Each main category has sub-types: for example, *ulnar* loops are those whose open ends point in the direction of the little finger of the same hand; *radial* loops point towards the thumb. In addition to the overall pattern, police measure other characteristics of a print such as the number of ridges, breaks or bridges between ridges, etc. When one takes into account all the various characteristics that a fingerprint may display, it is determined that no two fingerprints have ever been found to be precisely identical.

For the purposes of classification, forensic scientists use the

February 8, 1937

Mr. Julian Folvag,
Grenora, North Dakota.

Dear Sir:

    I have your letter of recent date in which you request
the fingerprint classification of one John Johnson. The
classification is as follows:
19) 11 R 10 19
    4 W 00 17.

    June 21, 1932, the Royal Canadian Mounted Police, at
Ottawa, Canada, requested that we furnish them with the
photograph of John Johnson, stating that they wished to
determine if the Albert Johnson who was killed in Canada was
the same as our John Johnson. The photograph and the
fingerprint classification was furnished to them at that
time, and under date of July 6, 1938, they replied that Albert
Johnson and John Johnson were without a doubt the same party.

        Yours very truly,

                                Warden

                  T. R. Bergstrom

Warden's letter stating that Albert Johnson and Johnny Johnson are
one and the same. At the time, this statement was an "error"! MON-
TANA STATE PRISON

primary patterns described above, as well as secondary and even
sub-secondary characteristics, in a rather complicated fashion.
They also assign a number to each pattern according to which
finger it is on. Together, these classification numbers make it
possible to file and retrieve fingerprint patterns easily—rather
as the numbers assigned to library books make it possible to
group them together by similarity but still be easily retrievable.

    Albert's left forefinger was a radial loop and his left middle

Typical specimens for each of the three main types of fingerprints.
TOM FIORENZA/NEWARK POLICE DEPT.

finger was an ulnar loop. In contrast, Johnny Johnson's left forefinger was a double loop whorl and his left middle finger was also a whorl pattern. One does not have to be an expert to ascertain that Albert's and John's prints were so completely different, there was no chance that the two men could be the same. So where was the "out" if there were any?

I prodded myself to look at things pragmatically. I could not let my emotions and "intuition" tell me that because I thought two men were one and the same, they actually were. If there was a catch in the case, I was hard put to find it. Fingerprints do not lie. I put my latest research into a box and stashed it away in a closet. But that did not keep me from mulling the thing over in my mind. Johnny Johnson's looks, his ancestry, vital statistics, and his modus operandi matched those of the man killed by the Mounties. Above all, the fact that I had commenced research on one end of the trail—with the photo of the dead trapper, and worked my way to the other end to a man matching Albert's description in North Dakota, whose trail led right back full circle to my beginning point in the north—all this seemed, in my opinion, to tip the scales in favour of my theory. Coincidence was one thing, but solid research was another. Analyzing a situation, working it out, and then coming up with a solution where you expect it to be, carries a bit more weight than a blind guess. But again, fingerprints do not lie. How could I *legitimately* reinterpret the fingerprint evidence to support my theory?

I moped over my dilemma in January, 1982, well aware that it was the fiftieth anniversary of the famous "war" between Albert Johnson and the Mounties. February 17, the anniversary of Albert's death, passed and I failed to come up with any original ideas regarding the fingerprints. March 1982 arrived and still no visions stirred me. Yet I was reluctant to let go of the Johnny Johnson theory.

I'm normally not a superstitious man—other than the odd little thing. I still won't mention a no-hit game if a pitcher has one going, but that is about the extent of it. March 9 rolled around. Headlines were made at the time by the fact that the "Jupiter Effect" was supposed to take place that day. This was the premise of a book written under the same title, in which giant cataclysms were predicted as the result of an unusual line-up of the planets of our solar system. I was aware that Albert Johnson was buried on March 9, 1932, and that Watson's memo pertaining to Albert's and Johnny's fingerprints was written on March 9, 1937. Half-kidding I said to my wife, Andrée, "All of the planets are in line tonight. Who knows, maybe Al will climb out of his grave and give me a sign." My wife looked at me with the usual degree of patronization she reserves for the "Mad Trapper obsession" and went on washing the dishes. Indulgently allowing for her lack of faith, I raided the fridge, took out a beer to help the Jupiter Effect along, and then laid out my Johnson file on the kitchen table. I separated Johnny Johnson's fingerprint card from the rest of the material and stared at it. I even shifted my gaze to the kitchen window and looked for the planets. All I could see was the blackness of heavy cloud cover, but I knew the celestial orbs were in line out there somewhere. I shuffled through more papers and came up with the descriptions of Albert's fingerprints. Of them only two were available and their nomenclature was limited to the patterns mentioned in the memo, a radial loop of the left forefinger, and an ulnar loop of the left middle finger. The fact that the memo mentioned no ridge counts of Albert's prints made it unnecessary for me to worry about them unless, of course, a full set of the dead man's prints were suddenly discovered. I mulled that over. I marvelled that the RCMP had stored volumes of material on the Albert Johnson case but had not kept what I considered *the* most important document of all, Albert's finger-prints, or at least their classification.

If the RCMP really wanted to find out some day who Albert was, it would seem that they would retain his fingerprints above everything else. Granted, almost everything gets destroyed sooner or later—the RCMP, like every other department of government, have to houseclean their files once in a while—or face the alternative of being buried in paper. But in this case destroying the fingerprints would not fit in with the fact that they had kept all the rest of the stuff. Why, out of all of the material, were the prints missing? Was it possible that they had not been destroyed or lost, but were still in existence, some-where else?

The RCMP had been co-operative with me throughout my research on two books I had written about subjects concerning their history,[5] but a nagging question presented itself—could there have been something about the fingerprints that perhaps only Watson himself knew?

I drew up a chart of Johnny Johnson's fingerprint patterns. Counting from one to ten, number one was the right thumb, two was the right forefinger, and so on, through the left hand. Underneath this I placed the patterns of Albert's as recorded in the memo.

	RIGHT					/	LEFT				
	1	2	3	4	5	/	6	7	8	9	10
J. J.	UL	RL	UL	W	UL		UL	W	W	W	UL
A. J.									RL	UL	

After staring glumly at the chart for a few moments, there seeped into my weary cerebrum the obvious fact that the pat-terns of Albert's *left* forefinger and *left* middle finger were the same as the equivalent digits on John's *right* hand. I did a double take. I had just finished reading a bulletin published by the International Association for Identification in which finger-print mix-ups were mentioned. *If Albert Johnson's prints had been*

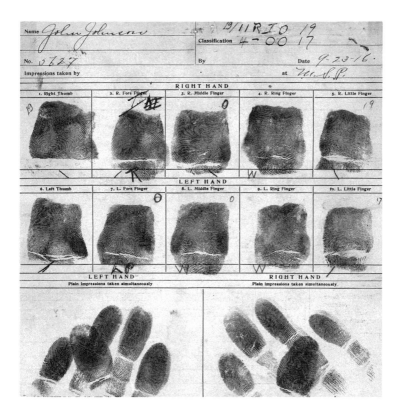

Johnny Johnson's fingerprints as supplied by Montana State Penitentiary. MONTANA STATE PENITENTIARY

transposed when they were taken it would explain the reason why he had never been identified as Johnny. Albert's classification would never have matched John's and, as a result, Watson, in all innocence, would have written as much to the wardens of the Montana State Penitentiary in 1932 and 1937. Yet they had had the evidence right there all along. Perhaps he later discovered the error which in turn poses a question impossible to ignore: *Could he have deliberately suppressed knowledge of the mistake?* It is impossible to read another person's mind on points like this without leaving oneself open to accusations of prejudice. If perchance Watson did not notice the transposition when he received the fingerprint classification of Johnny in 1932, and then five years later did notice it when he was sent the actual prints, one could sympathize with him if he failed to note the error. The Mounties had "got their man" and there was no actual need to establish Albert Johnson's identity. Maybe he would have decided to let the sleeping dog lie and keep the mongrel—the fingerprints—under lock and key.[6]

CHAPTER 13

THE NET TIGHTENS

STYMIED BECAUSE of the "fingerprints that disappeared"—the ultimate bulwark in a researcher's obstacle course—I switched my tack and decided to send photos of Johnny Johnson to those people in the north who had met Albert Johnson and/or Arthur Nelson. Many of Johnny's neighbours had credibly identified Albert's photo as Johnny. It seemed worthwhile to see if Albert's most credible acquaintances would do the reverse: identify Johnny's photo as Albert.

I made half a dozen photocopies of John's pictures from the Lincoln County, Wyoming, jail record in which his left profile photo was at left, and his full face photo was at right, and mailed them out. I have to admit that this approach was a far from decisive one. I had delayed for several years, for fear the response would be negative—more from a subliminal timidity than a conscious one, but the effect had been long procrastination.

One of the first individuals I contacted was Tom Smith. He was a power plant operator near Whitehorse when I originally interviewed him in the sixties. Tom had told me he'd met Nelson at Teslin in 1927, and he identified the man in the Ross River photo as the man he had encountered. Several years after my interview Smith had retired and returned to his hometown of Teslin, a predominantly Indian hamlet nestled on the shores of a scenic lake of the same name, about 120 miles southeast of Whitehorse. My wife and I had once visited Tom and his wife, the former Lilly Fox, at their pleasant little home only a stone's throw from an arm of the lake. They were centrally located for Tom's many activities, which included a position as supervisor of the Teslin canoe factory, as well as that of an instructor in the art of snowshoe making. Tom Smith is considered by other members of the Teslin band the finest crafter of snowshoes in that part of the north country. During our visit he showed us the exact spot where he had met Nelson when the stranger camped on the shores of the lake in 1927. It was less than 100 yards from his cabin.

Visualizing Tom and Lilly at their place, I mailed off the photos and in a short time had received Tom's reply. Of the two shots I sent, Smith identified the left profile in particular as the man he had met at the lake so many years before: "I received your letter along with the photos enclosed. The person in the photo is the guy I recognize. I wrote a note to show which photo I recognize. It is the photo shot from the side."

Photo perusal is a precarious way to establish identity at best. The reasons range through a whole gamut of "probables", from the angle at which a photo is taken to the memory and credibility of the viewer. We all know, too, that some persons' memories are better than others'. There are detectives trained in the art of identification who can peruse a reef of photos and later, with only a glance, recall every individual.

Instructors of courses intended to improve one's memory with respect to identification point out there are a number of factors that help one's ability for recall. *Interest*, for example, makes a difference. If a man and a woman are attracted to each other across the proverbial crowded room, they have no trouble in remembering what the other looks like. It goes without saying that if there were no attraction there would be no memory in such an instance. *Conditions* have a strong influence on identification. If a formal party is given where those in attendance are in evening attire, and one couple shows up dressed like tramps, they will not soon be forgotten. *Location* is equally important. A person bedecked in the flowing robes of a Bedouin strolling down a street in Moose Jaw would presumably attract plenty of attention and be long remembered.

Letter from Tom Smith identifying mug shot of Johnny Johnson as Albert Johnson. TOM SMITH

The ramblings of Albert Johnson/Arthur Nelson fit into the "location" category. One must first peruse a map of northern British Columbia, the Yukon Territory, and the Northwest Territories to really appreciate the utter isolation of those areas during the period that he was wandering through them. There was no Alaska Highway then. Airplanes were so rare that entire communities would turn out en masse to see one when it landed. There were no train connections other than a 110-mile railroad from the coast at Skagway to Whitehorse. There was no

road from Whitehorse to Dawson City. The Dempster Highway from Dawson City to the mouth of the Mackenzie River
was not even a dream between 1927 and 1932. The entire
region from Dease Lake, B.C. to Fort McPherson, N.W.T.—
over a million square miles—had less than 10,000 people in it,
the majority of whom lived in only a few communities. Two of
the largest towns in the north country today, Inuvik and Yellowknife, were not even in existence in 1932! Over half of the
residents of that part of North America were native Indian
people, many of whom still resided in the bush.

Therefore, when a tow-headed stranger the likes of Johnson/
Nelson showed up, he stood out not only because he was a
newcomer, but also because he was a white man in an area
primarily occupied by Indians. Thus when Tom Smith, a Tlin-
git Indian, met the stranger on the shore of the lake after he had
suddenly emerged on foot seemingly from nowhere, the conditions were right for Smith to remember him. Another point
worth emphasizing is that Tom Smith had been raised as a
trapper and a hunter. By the very nature of his occupation,
Smith was trained to keep a sharp eye out for detail whether it
was the tip of a willow that had been nipped off by a passing
moose or the intricacies of reading a faint pawprint left in the
snow by a prowling wolf.

Therefore all of the requisites were present for Smith to have
recalled the man he met—the isolation of the community, the
difference of race, Smith's wilderness training. There was also
the fact that the newcomer toted a 100-pound pack topped off
with two bear skins that he used for sleeping robes; that was an
uncommon sight even for that wilderness area.

For all of the preceding reasons, I would credit Tom Smith as
a witness whose testimony was of extreme value. If his recollections coincided with other persons of equal reliability, the case
for Albert Johnson and John Johnson being one and the same
man would be that much stronger.

Next, I sent copies of the Johnny Johnson photos to John
Robert at Fort McPherson. Robert had identified the Ross
River photo as the man he had met at Fort McPherson. As

mentioned, Robert sold supplies to Albert Johnson on several occasions while working as a clerk at the Northern Traders store in 1931. John has been a pillar of the Fort McPherson community for many years. A tee-totaller, John is of that generation of Indian people—like Joe Henry—who led nomadic lives in their early youth, trapping and hunting in the vast wilderness of the Richardson and Ogilvie mountains.

James Andre, his son-in-law, and with whom John lives, replied on his behalf. He wrote:

"I showed him [John Robert] the picture and he said it was Albert Johnson. He points to the picture on the left column as him—the one with the side view."

Thus the two men, Tom Smith and John Robert, who lived over five hundred miles apart and were unacquainted, had unhesitatingly identified Johnny as Albert. A curious note was that, of the two photos of Johnny that I sent to the men, both had zeroed in on the left profile. There must have been some characteristic in Johnny's left profile that was distinctive enough to make his profile memorable. This may have been his blond hair or the cowlick, which are noticeable in the left profile but not in the full face shot because he was wearing a cowboy hat.

Another link was forged in the chain of steps Johnson took on his long solitary journey when he met Arthur John at Ross River. I sent the photos of Johnny to Dick Craft, who lives at Ross. The pictures of Johnny were taken twelve years before Arthur John met him in 1927. Craft showed them to Arthur John, who had been fifteen or sixteen when he had known Johnson in the late twenties. He said they looked like the man he had known, only the man of the photos was a lot younger, and that he had known him as Dick Johnson.

There was another witness to be consulted. John Robert, who had tried to sell Johnson the outboard motor, never saw the body of Albert Johnson, but I knew someone who had, and under circumstances so weird, he would almost certainly have never forgotten what he saw. If this man identified the photos of Johnny as the dead man, Albert Johnson, it would complete the chain in establishing his identity through visual recollection. This man was Paul Nieman, whom I mentioned earlier as having identified the photo of Phil Branstrom.

Nieman was a man with an incredible memory. Working solely from recall, at eighty-four years of age he sat down and wrote out a 50,000-word autobiography in longhand. His retention was almost total for names, places, and dates.

He emigrated to Canada from Germany as a youth, settling in Alberta. A few years later, bitten by the trapping bug, he set out for the north country by travelling down the Mackenzie River, finally coming to rest at Fort McPherson in 1927. During the flu epidemic that swept the area soon after he arrived, Nieman helped minister to the Indians and is remembered even today for helping the sick.

Nieman heard about good trapping country on the west side of the Richardson Mountains from Fort McPherson, and moved over there to set up a trap line in 1930. Paul was trapping on the Bell River when Wop May flew over him during the manhunt for Johnson. Curious as to what was up, he mushed to the trading post at La Pierre House farther up the Bell in order to find out. It was dark when he arrived, and to his surprise he found many members of the posse there including Frank Jackson, proprietor of the trading post. Jackson told him what had happened and that the Mad Trapper's body had been placed atop the post's food cache, which was a platform about fifteen feet off the ground. He asked Paul if he had known "Albert Johnson", the man they had killed, and Nieman replied he could not answer the question unless he looked at the body. So he propped a ladder against the platform and climbed up to have a look. When he reached the cache, he peeled back the canvas that covered the man's face and realized he had forgotten to bring a lantern or a flashlight with him. He pulled his matches from his pocket and hesitated briefly, wondering what the man looked like.

Finally, he struck a match, the burst of light from which revealed the countenance of the dead man. Paul Nieman was not a man easily shocked, but he said Johnson's looks were even "rougher" than he thought they would be, though not so bad that the man was unrecognizable. Nieman carefully studied the cadaver's features, striking half a dozen more matches before satisfying himself that he did not know him. He turned the canvas back over the body and retreated down the ladder.

I went to Nieman's place and presented him with photos of John Johnson, at the same time asking him if he thought John and Albert were the same. Nieman was a meticulous man and studied the photos carefully before he answered me.

"Yes," he said, "that's the guy I looked at on the cache at La Pierre House. The left photo is the one that looks the most like him."

"You said the left photo. The one from the side?"

"Yes," he replied, "why?"

I informed him of the similar observations of John Robert and Tom Smith, and he seemed quite pleased that his recollections coincided with theirs.

Paul Nieman had not returned to Fort McPherson for several decades, so there was no chance he had been talking with John Robert, and his acquaintance with Tom Smith was at best a fleeting one. Nieman's observations were his own, and not influenced by anyone else. They supported the recollections of Smith, Robert, and of Arthur John. As far as those witnesses were concerned, the man killed by the Mounties was Johnny Johnson.

Then, to my surprise, another link was added to the other end of the chain again when I received a letter from Dick Hickman, North Dakota law man and editor of the *North Dakota Peace Officer's Journal*. I had sent him a copy of my first book, which had piqued his interest further. He had discovered that a woman named Lena Stanley, aged ninety-two, of Williston, North Dakota, had known the Johnson family and she identified the photo taken at Ross River as that of Johnny Johnson.

I visited Williston where Hickman introduced me to Mrs. Stanley, a remarkable woman at any age. Keen of wit and sharp of eye, she, like the famous American artist "Grandma" Moses, had become a proficient painter of oils beginning at the age of eighty-seven. To do that, her vision had to be good, and judging by the excellence of her work, it was.

Lena explained her connection with the Johnson family, and gave some insight into Johnny Johnson's personality during our conversation. She said she became friends with John's sister, Olga, and mother, Petra, in the fall of 1915 when she worked as a cook on a threshing crew at the Johnson farm. An early snowstorm had halted the harvest that year, and she spent some time with the Johnsons.

Lena had heard about the Medicine Lake bank hold-up and learned more about it from Olga one day when they were riding the Johnsons' horses. At Olga's suggestion, she rubbed her hand over the flank of the horse she was riding and felt the buckshot under its skin. Olga told her it came from the shotgun blasts the posse had fired when it tried to stop Magnor and John after the hold-up. That was as close as Lena would get to the raw nature of the real wild west, and that was close enough! At that time, no one in the Johnson family knew the whereabouts of John, and Magnor was being held at Deer Lodge. Olga was the only child left at home and the burden of supporting her aging father and mother was a heavy one. According to Lena the fact that neither Petra nor Anders could speak English further complicated the family's poor circumstances.

Lena said that after John returned home in 1918, he built a new barn and did his best to resurrect the fortunes of the family, but he left in 1920 and she never met him again after that. During the time he was home, she saw him on occasion at dances held at a school situated across the road from where she and her first husband lived. (She had married a veteran when he returned from the First World War in 1919.) Lena said that Johnny never danced with anyone, was always alone, and rarely if ever spoke.

"He had a way of standing," she told us and imitated him, "in which he looked down. He would glance up with his eyes yet not move his head. He was just plain shy. The picture you have at Ross River with his hair parted and down in the face is him." The observation coincided with the recollection of Laura Sulli-

Lena Stanley, 92, demonstrates stance of Johnny Johnson who typically looked at the ground or peered out from under his eyebrows.
DICK HICKMAN

van Moi who met "Arthur Nelson" at Keno City in 1931. Laura, an impressionable girl of seventeen, was struck by Johnson's good looks, and shyness. She said, "He would look at the ground and avoid your eyes." Her father had accompanied

REGISTRATION CARD

| SERIAL NUMBER | 2246 | | A | ORDER NUMBER | 1990 |

1   John   Conrad   Johnson.

(First name)   (Middle name)   ast name)

2 PERMANENT HOME ADDRESS: Grenora   Williams   N.D.

(No.)   (Street or R. F. D. No.)   (City or town)   (County)   (State)

Age in Years	Date of Birth		
20	July	13	1898
	(Month)	(Day)	(Year)

RACE

| White | Negro | Oriental | Indian Citizen | Indian Noncitizen |
| 5 ✓ | 6 | 7 | 8 | 9 |

U. S. CITIZEN			ALIEN	
Native Born	Naturalized	Citizen by Father's Naturalization Before Registrant's Majority	Declarant	Non-declarant
10	11	12 ✓	13	14

15 If not a citizen of the U. S., of what nation are you a citizen or subject?

| PRESENT OCCUPATION | EMPLOYER'S NAME |
| 16 Farmer | 17 |

18 PLACE OF EMPLOYMENT OR BUSINESS:

(No.)   (Street or R. F. D. No.)   (City or town)   (County)   (State)

| NEAREST RELATIVE | Name | 19 Andrew C. Johnson. |
| | Address | 20 |

(No.)   (Street or R. F. D.)   (City or town)   (County)   (State)

I AFFIRM THAT I HAVE VERIFIED ABOVE ANSWERS AND THAT THEY ARE TRUE

P. M. G. O.
Form No. 1 (Red)   John Conrad Johnson   (OVER)

Johnny Johnson's draft registration, signed in 1918, after he returned home from his Wyoming and Montana imprisonment. This is the only existing document where Johnny appears to have told the truth about himself. U.S. DEPT. OF JUSTICE

Nelson on the trail for a few days. The impressions of the two women, who were close to the same age when they met Johnny, were remarkably similar.

Lena added that Johnny was known to be the best revolver and rifle shot in the area. "He could hit a target while riding at full gallop firing a pistol from underneath a horse's neck," she said.

Mrs. Stanley closed with another anecdote about John Johnson that indicated he never mended his ways, at least while she knew him: "He sold a team of horses to my sister and brother-in-law before he left. They found out later the horses had been stolen."

CHAPTER 14

ANOTHER RUN AT EXHUMATION

A N OLD FRIEND who managed the *Yukon Indian News*, Malcolm Dawson, put me on contract to do some work for the
newspaper in the fall of 1984. While so employed I met Janet
Wilson from Yellowknife, capital of the Northwest Territories.
In the meantime I had not given up on the idea of exhuming
Albert Johnson. Hearing where Janet was from, I explained my
mission and asked her if she could recommend a lawyer in that
city who might be able to help me. She suggested Don Cooper,
the senior partner of a law firm there. Though a relatively young
man then in his mid-thirties, Don had fifteen years' experience
in the Arctic and knew most of the Northwest Territories as if it
were his own backyard.

I wrote to Cooper on May 15, 1985, and summarized the
steps I had taken since I had first sought an exhumation of
Johnson's body in 1981. Adding that experts had now reviewed
the fingerprints, I asked him if he would help me steer the
application through the legal maze of the government. I also
mentioned that I was no Ernest Hemingway, and that my funds
were quite limited.

Cooper, a punctual man, responded immediately. He suggested if I did not want to be turned down again by the
Coroner, that affidavits would have to be obtained from the
experts to whom I had referred. Don demonstrated he was not
without a sense of humour when he appended his advice with
the comment that he was no F. Lee Bailey (the American attorney whose fees occasionally reached astronomical figures). He

agreed to take on the job for a minimal retainer and volunteered to donate some of his time to the project, citing as his reasons a general interest in history and a particular fascination with the Johnson mystery.

Looking back, I do not think either one of us would have taken another step if we had realized then that two long years would pass before we obtained a decision. However, just undertaking the process was advantageous, if for no other reason than that I was nudged in the direction of more research.

I immediately called Tom Zaruba, a detective in Juneau, Alaska, and the only private eye I knew of within five hundred miles of Whitehorse. Zaruba, like Cooper, was another history buff. He had read with interest the material I sent to him concerning the contradictory aspects of Albert Johnson's fingerprints. He agreed to write up his conclusions on the subject and said he would sign an affidavit attesting to his findings.

Zaruba's qualifications were impressive. After a seven-year stint in the army he went to work for the Alaska State Troopers where he served as a detective and eventually became supervisor of the general investigation unit. After ten years with them, he was appointed chief security officer for the Alaska Division of Corrections, serving in that position until he saw an opportunity to work for himself. He set up an office as a private detective in Juneau, Alaska. In a short time he acquired many more clients than he could handle. Obtaining his services was a stroke of luck for me.

Yet another professional, recommended by Zaruba, was fingerprint expert Clay Brookshire. Also a resident of Juneau, he had over ten years' experience in the fingerprint section of the Alaska Department of Public Safety. While in that position he testified as an expert witness in scores of cases.

The statement filed by Zaruba summarized the views of both men regarding the confusion over the prints and corroborated my layman's observations on the subject. Zaruba carefully laid out his deposition:

Now as to the dissimilar fingerprint information cited

in the letter dated January 20, 1982 from R. L. James, Chief Coroner, Northwest Territories:

In his letter, Mr. James cites a memo of March 9, 1937 from the RCMP-DCI indicating Albert Johnson's post mortem fingerprint patterns have a radial loop on the left forefinger and an ulnar loop on the left middle finger.

While John Johnson's left forefinger is recorded and verified as a double loop and his left middle finger is a whorl pattern, his right forefinger is a radial loop and his right middle finger is an ulnar loop.

I would submit to you that when taking into consideration the circumstances under which the Albert Johnson prints were obtained (post mortem of a rigored and frozen subject during field conditions), the relatively new usage of fingerprints as an identification medium, and the limited training and techniques available to law enforcement personnel in 1932, the transposition of left and right hand post mortem prints could have been quite possible.

By way of explanation, the state of the art method of taking post mortem fingerprints as late as the 1960s was accomplished with the use of an inking pad, finger spoon and print strips. Absent the proper equipment, prints were often obtained by using any ink and paper available at the time as a field expedient.

Transcending back to the 1930s in the Yukon, it is probably a logical assumption that Albert Johnson's prints were obtained by one of these two methods.

In the first instance, if strips were utilized, it is quite possible that the prints were transposed due to a labeling error or the use of the left strip on the right hand or vice versa. This can happen quite easily if an individual with limited experience or training prints a corpse.

Classifiable fingerprints are difficult to obtain if the body is rigored or frozen and are most probably taken from the front of the body instead of from behind the body as is the case with a live subject. This tends to disorient a

taker of limited experience, and could cause the mislabel-
ling or transposition of the print strips.

In the second instance, if the prints were taken on plain
paper the same possibilities exist coupled with the additional risks of administrative errors.

Even today, with tremendous gains in technology and
increased levels of training required of police officials, the
transposition of individual fingerprints is not an uncommon occurrence, particularly during the taking of post
mortem prints.

Zaruba's observations were doubly pertinent in view of the
recollections of pilot Wop May who toted Johnson's body back
to Aklavik after the trapper was killed. He said:

So Jack [Bowen, his mechanic] and I loaded Johnson's
body . . . into the Bellanca, and we hopped off for Aklavik.
Our return flight was made without incident, and soon we
were back at the post and the Inspector was fingerprinting
the dead man for identification purposes. That proved to
be a horrible task too, for Johnson's body was frozen hard
as iron and his hands were clamped like claws as he had
died clutching his rifle in his last fight.[1]

Since pictures taken of the body show it suspended from a
rope in the blubber shed at Aklavik, it is safe to assume the
prints were lifted as suggested by Zaruba—taken from the
front rather than in the customary way.

And, since the fingerprints were taken twice,[2] no other conclusion can be drawn but that there was considerable difficulty,
and perhaps some sort of a dilemma regarding the prints of
Albert Johnson.

Supporting the "dilemma" aspect of the fingerprints is a
letter I received from retired Detective Sergeant Ralph H.
Godfrey of the Oakland, California, Police Department where
for many years he served in the fingerprint section. Answering
my query about the methods employed in taking prints from

deceased persons, he wrote, "I've had considerable experience taking fingerprints from cadavers in the County Morgue under all kinds of conditions. I can tell you it is an art in itself . . . I would suspect the RCMP in 1932 under those crude conditions would not be versed in many . . . print recovery procedures, and having tried a couple of times, had to give it up, and any prints they did get would probably be unidentifiable, and smeared, and unclassifiable."

Even these letters don't mention all the possibilities for error. You'll notice if you study the fingerprint cards that the same fingers for each hand are above and below each other. Now, if you put your hand onto the right-hand card, you'll see that the finger places on the card are in the same order as the fingers are on the hand. But if you put your *left* hand on the print card for that hand, you will see that the fingerprints are in *reverse* order to the order on your hand. The classification of the fingerprints, however, is based on the way the patterns flow *on the hand*, not on the print card. Thus loops on the card for a left hand that point towards the thumb print are still *ulnar* loops, not *radial*, because on the real hand they would point towards the little finger.

Spurred on by such puzzling factors, I mailed the necessary material to Don Cooper. The riddle could be solved if Albert Johnson were disinterred. It was as simple as that.

Cooper forwarded the papers to Sheldon Hebb, Chief Coroner, since James' retirement, who nimbly sidestepped the request by stating the case would not come under his jurisdiction because Johnson was killed in the Yukon Territory, not in the Northwest Territories. Hebb suggested that the application be submitted to the Registrar of Vital Statistics, Mrs. Vicky Hickey, and went ahead and forwarded the documents to her office.

In order to reinforce my position, I drew up several extensive charts that compared the physical characteristics and the modus operandi of the two Johnsons. Cooper also sent these to the Registrar.

The fact that my research papers were now in the hands of the registrar, however, did not mean that I had nothing to do. Vital Statistics insisted that I obtain approval of the hamlet council in Aklavik before they would approve the project.

I began a correspondence with Knute Hansen, manager of the hamlet, and Tom Arey, the mayor. They agreed to bring the idea before the council, but first they said they would need as much information as I could provide on the matter. To make my presentation as convincing as possible, I put together a twenty-nine page indexed dissertation. Included in it were a capsulized statement about my research by Don Cooper, letters from people who had known one or the other of the men and identified John and Albert as one and the same, comments of the detectives, fingerprints, and all of the comparisons I had drawn up. I made nine copies and sent them to the hamlet.

I must admit that I was not optimistic about the potential success of the new presentation, mainly because the earlier one had been turned down. I was somewhat astonished, then, when the council took a bold step and approved the plan by a vote of five to one with one abstention. The hamlet forwarded their approval in a letter to Cooper which he presented to the Registrar of Vital Statistics. This meant—as far as I could see it—that all of the Registrar's demands had been met.

Council meetings everywhere in Canada are public, and when possible the media covers these exercises in democracy. Media people regularly reported on the meetings of the Aklavik council, and quickly spotted the news interest inherent in the exhumation request when it was brought up. In a short time it became a national news item. Having been a journalist myself, I recognized the romance of the story, but I also knew the more publicity the project received, the less chance there would be of my achieving what I had set out to do. For one, the Registrar had not yet come up with a decision on the application, and for another, the cemetery in which Johnson was buried—almost in the centre of Aklavik—was almost too visible. There were bound to be residents who would object to the exhumation for reasons ranging from personal convenience to aesthetic ones. The more the project was blown up in the media the greater would be the opposition. And that is exactly what happened.

As attention on the proposal grew it served to spur an element of opposition in Aklavik. This included some of the local elders, the Anglican church, and the newly elected leader of the Indian band. I wrote to these parties and the only one who responded was Reverend Chesterton who underlined his objections in a forthright manner. In my ignorance I had assumed that Reverend Dixon was still in residence at Aklavik, and I had not informed Chesterton, his replacement, about the project.

The objections of the local groups were voiced to the Minister of Justice in Yellowknife, who overruled the hamlet council and turned down the application. My error had been in assuming that the Aklavik Council represented the entire community.[3]

I was certainly disappointed by this turn of events, but not overly so. What bothered me more was the fact that so much time and effort had been expended on the part of my associates, particularly Don Cooper, and to a lesser degree, Tom Zaruba and Clay Brookshire. I felt, in a sense, that I had wasted their time in my vain attempt to exhume Johnson. The same held true with Arey, Hansen, and the hamlet council. They had put themselves on the line in a real effort to clear up one of the Arctic's great mysteries. They had respected my proposal and now were left with nothing more than a residue of paper representing a researcher's crumpled dreams. However, as the old saying goes, it is an ill wind that blows no good. If I had not been required to satisfy the wants of Cooper with respect to Vital Statistics and the Coroner, I would not have accumulated the data in the first place.

One of the queries inspired by Coroner James' earlier revelations on the fingerprint patterns was a letter I wrote to the *R.C.M.P. Quarterly*, the results of which now make a prospective exhumation, if it ever happens, even more interesting. In my note I asked the readers if they could contribute any information about Johnson's fingerprints.

Alec Green, a retired RCMP staff sergeant, wrote the follow-ing to me from his retirement home in Walnut Creek, Califor-nia:

"I was in the Force at the time of the 'Mad Trapper' incident, and later was stationed with Corporal King, one of the boys shot by Johnson. As I recall what King told me, Johnson had no identifiable fingerprints as he either burned them off with acid or scraped them down on rough stone. I do not know if there is an official record to this effect."

I think it would be safe to say that Green would not report King's declaration if it had not in fact been made. Similarly, one can assume that King, who packed the fingerprints of Albert Johnson with him when he flew to Edmonton with pilot Punch Dickins on February 21, 1932, would not make a spurious statement to Green.

Assuming that Green's recollection is credible, then, his letter underscored my feelings that the fingerprints were a key to the mystery. One does not have to be a detective to see the obvious. A man does not destroy the epidermis of the tips of his fingers without a reason. The only conclusion that can be drawn from this is that Albert Johnson was a criminal in the profes-sional sense. This means that the man buried at Aklavik was, or had been, an active and regular participant in organized crimi-nal activities.

Looking at it more closely: a man would destroy the skin of his fingertips for two reasons, one being the fear of detection for a crime already committed; the other, for detection of a crime he was *going* to commit. The seriousness of the commit-ted or contemplated crime would determine it.

A dime-store thief would not go through the painful experi-ence of having the flesh of his fingers chemically or surgically altered, whereas a gunman involved in the internecine battles of the underworld, bank robberies, and assassinations might undertake such an operation. In fact, in the late twenties and early thirties, destroying one's fingerprints became almost en-demic among the notorious crooks of North America, despite the fact that the operation itself made them more susceptible than ever to the sharp eyes of law men because of the connotation that went along with the scarred fingers. This would certainly have been visible to Inspector Watson when he received the prints from up north in 1932, but for reasons I can only now speculate on, he may have chosen to ignore this.

I must answer the inevitable question: were John and Albert the same man? Taking a cold, objective look at the vital statistics, modus operandi, and the history of the men, it would be difficult to come to any conclusion other than an affirmative one. Giving additional credence to this are the particulars they did *not* have, such as operation scars or outstanding marks or abrasions. The one exception with regard to this category was a mole listed for Albert Johnson two inches to the left of his spine in the mid lumbar region as opposed to a birthmark listed for Johnny Johnson on the "median link" at the centre of his back. Even in this we see the difference is more a matter of semantics than an actual discrepancy.

The photos deserve special attention. First, artist Dunleavy's sketches of a healthy Johnson based on the death photos should be examined carefully. Though Dunleavy's sketches were drawn with no knowledge of photos taken of Johnny Johnson, they are remarkably similar: the tuft of hair at the back of the head; the cowlick over the right eye; the heavy eyelids and similarly shaped eyebrows; the shape of the head; the nostrils; the upper and lower lips and area of the mouth. Conversely, the dissimilar points can be easily explained by the condition of Albert when he was killed. The left ear was either striated by frostbite or damaged in some other way. A beard covered the chin and made it look "stronger" than it actually was. The cleft in the chin is only partially visible because of the beard, and the nose appears shorter because of the low angle of the photo.

A crucial test of the author's thesis comes in comparing the various photos and sketches uncovered during the years of research. Almost all witnesses questioned reported a likeness between the side views

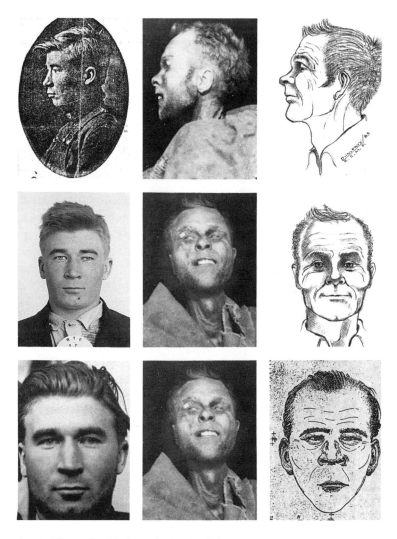

(top). The tuft of hair at the back of the head is present in both, as is the front cowlick. Note the heavy lids and the slight bend of the nose to the right (middle). The left ear of each appears to protrude more than the right. The proportions of the nose, mouth, and eyes are the same. The Identikit sketch, while diverging in some points from Dunleavy's sketches, shows striking similarities to the maturer Johnson during his San Quentin days.

(On following two pages): The close-ups of Johnny and Albert show the slightly enlarged right nostril. The cross-referencing of such personal features makes the identification virtually a certitude.

Comparing Johnny's mug shot with Albert's brings out a few points that Dunleavy missed. Close inspection reveals that Albert's nose was bent slightly to the right (or that the right

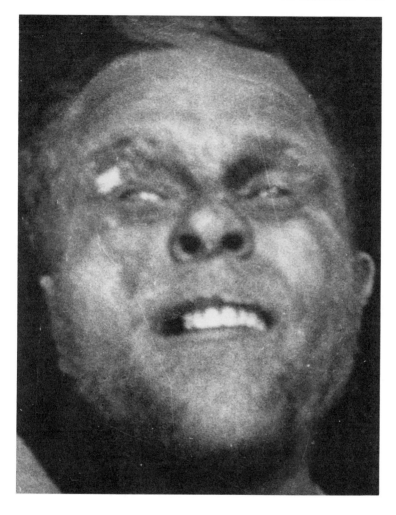

nostril was slightly longer than the left); and that his left ear protruded more than his right ear did. These abnormalities are readily visible in Johnny's picture. In addition, the left eye appears to be slightly out of sync with the right in Johnny's photo. This also may be detected, though less obviously so, in the death picture of Albert. It is these very small but unique

DESCRIPTION OF CONVICT

STATE PENITENTIARY, RAWLINS, WYOMING,

........June 15, 1915........ ....,x19x......

Secretary State Board of Charities and Reform:

The following is a descriptive report of William Hoffner Convict delivered at this

Penitentiary ....June 7, 1915.... ,x19x..., by.. S, Ed Manson Sheriff.. ....

Registered number..**2210**. .... ---

Name ....;.............WILLIAM HOFFNER ....

Where Convicted and Sentenced.............Kemmerer Wyo......................

County of .... Lincoln .... Term of Court........Mat 1915....... ....

Date of Sentence.....................June 4, 1915.................................

Length of Sentence..... ....12 to 18 Months............ .. ..

Place of Confinement—Wyoming State Penitentiary, Rawlins, Wyoming.

Crime...............Stealing live stock ....

Sex.......Male....... ...,; Age. ....19................. , Nativity...Nowhere ....

Occupation...Cowpuncher ......, Height .5- 8 3/4 ...., Weight ...144.............lbs.

Color ....White.............. ...., Complexion...Med Florid ....

Hair.....Light Chestnut.... ...., Eyes.... Blue........... . ...

Has Wife..no............ .., Parents....none..............., Children...---...............

Religion.......Lutheran................., Habits of Life....Moderate....................

Education......3 Years................, Parent's Address.....none....................

.... (. . . .

....

Marks, Scars and General Remarks..Spot scar joint left elbow................ .....

....Large wart palm of right hand. Large brown birthmark on median line

....center of back. Long cut scar lower left leg,..........................

....

....-.... . ...

Wyoming State Penitentiary registration form. WYOMING STATE
PENITENTIARY

characteristics that make it all but impossible to avoid the conclusion that Albert and Johnny were one and the same person.

John disappeared from the lives of those close to him in 1923 and never was heard from again. Albert, of course, had to come from somewhere, and the cross-referencing of identification of his photos goes a long way toward substantiating the fact that he came from North Dakota, and was, in fact, Johnny Johnson. The two were identified as the same from photos, even by people—such as his mother—who would have wanted to believe the opposite.

One final bit of evidence seems to capture the essence of Albert and Johnny Johnson. Oddly prophetic, it was an entry written on John's records in the Wyoming State Penitentiary. Dated June 15, 1915, under the title *Description of Convict* and sandwiched between "Crime—Stealing livestock" and "Occupation—Cowpuncher" was the notation "Nativity—Nowhere".

Asked about such an odd entry, Dick Hickman of the North Dakota CIB responded that he had never seen such a reference in his twenty years as a law enforcement officer.

Prophetic? On page 47 of my first book on Albert Johnson written in 1972, long before I ever heard of Johnny Johnson, I had written: "It was as if he [Albert Johnson] had come from nowhere, and was a 'non-person'."

After looking for twenty years, I had literally found the man from "Nowhere".

EPILOGUE

RICHARD MARTIN'S RECOLLECTION that when some Indians at Eagle, Alaska, met Albert Johnson camped along the Yukon River, he "was reading about himself in the newspaper" led me to wonder whether the loner could have been perusing the sensationalist articles about the murder of Alfred ("Jake") Lingle, reporter for the Chicago *Tribune*, on June 9, 1930 as discussed earlier. Since the man the Indians claimed to have met was not involved socially with anyone in the Yukon Territory or Alaska other than the occasional trapper or fur trader he encountered, a news story concerning him would have had to originate elsewhere. Furthermore, *if* Johnson was the Chicago triggerman, one item in the Lingle story would have caused him special concern: the description of the killer as reported by eye witnesses to the slaying. I quote the newspapers: "He is described as five feet ten inches tall, age about thirty years, weight 160 pounds, with light brown hair and blue eyes"—exactly the general description that fit Johnson.

Early in this book I said that for Johnson to have been involved in the Lingle affair, underworld connections would have been imperative. If Albert Johnson and Johnny Johnson were one and the same, those links could have existed. First, the fact that Johnny spent almost six years of his youth in several of the toughest penitentiaries in North America; and second, that Albert, in true gangland style, "burned" his fingertips, and in the mode of underworld desperados, had not one iota of identification on him when he was killed.

The man who was eventually tried and convicted for the
Lingle killing, Leo Brothers (whom Johnson resembled),
swore he did not do it, and the jury must have had doubts for he
was given only fourteen years with seven off for good behaviour. In those days any sentence less than the death penalty for
murder was virtually an exoneration. The ongoing controversy
over who killed the newspaperman evolved as the title of a book
written by a reporter who investigated the slaying, *Who Killed
Jake Lingle, and Why?*

Could that man have been Albert Johnson? The general
physical descriptions of the two men matched and so did estimates of their age. Brothers, however, was five feet eleven
inches, thirty-one years of age, weighed 178 pounds, had
medium chestnut hair, and was described as portly. In 1930,
Albert, if he were Johnny, would have been thirty-one or almost
thirty-two. The murder weapon was traced to a sporting goods
store in downtown Chicago, the proprietors of which dealt
frequently with Canadian bootleggers.[2] In addition, Al
Capone, to whom the murder victim was considerably in debt
and whom Lingle may have double-crossed in a race track deal,
according to some of his acquaintances, had many "associates"
in Canada. Could Capone have summoned a hit man from
Canada to do the job? The tactic was commonly employed when
the mob wanted a man "rubbed out". Bringing in an individual
from the Dominion was a theory worth entertaining.

Supporting this idea is the fact that Chicagoans formed a
large percentage of tourists to the Yukon Territory each
summer. Virtually inaccessible at other times of the year, the
Territory was easy to reach in the summer. It took only three
days by train to Seattle. From there travellers had two options.
One alternative took them by ship directly to Skagway, Alaska,
thence by train to Whitehorse, Yukon Territory, and from there
downriver by steamboat to Dawson City. This took about a
week, or ten full days from Chicago.

Photograph of Leo V. Brothers, who was convicted of the murder of Jack Lingle. ILLINOIS STATE ARCHIVES

Passengers taking the other option sailed to Seward, Alaska, and there entrained on the Alaska Railroad for Anchorage, Nenana, and Fairbanks. Those desiring to go on to the Yukon Territory left the train at Nenana. Paddlewheelers then took them down the Tanana River and up the Yukon River to complete the trip. This took about two weeks. Consequently, a man fleeing Chicago on June 9 could have been back in the Yukon Territory by June 23 at the latest, or the 19th at the earliest. This would have allowed more than enough time for Johnson, if he were the hit man, to have made it back to the Yukon by way of the Seward route—which would have brought him into the Eagle, Alaska, area—and also fits in with the *Dawson City News* item of August 7 that enumerated Dick Johnson as a passenger heading upriver to Fort Selkirk, where he would change boats to take the smaller draught *Yukon Rose* to Ross River.

Another piece of evidence pops up here that matches Johnson's perambulations. Alex Biederman, manager of the Northern Commercial Company store in Eagle, sent a radiogram to RCMP headquarters in Dawson City on February 18, 1932, the day after Albert Johnson was killed. "Man answering Johnson's description stole one revolver, rifle, and ammunition twenty months ago from Charlie Creek. Please send description of guns and ammunition used by Johnson. This may clear up mystery down here. Send information collect." (By "down here" Biederman meant downriver from Dawson City.)

Counting backwards twenty months from February 17, 1932, puts Johnson at Charlie Creek in mid-July of 1930. Charlie Creek was about one hundred miles downriver from Eagle (i.e. north of Eagle), and thus it was also well within the realm of possibility for him to have been at Charlie Creek and still have reached Dawson City in time to appear on the passenger list on the date he did. Biederman's note also serves to back up the statement of Indians in that vicinity that they had met such a man in the first place.

One other point should be noted: the persistent feeling on the part of Constable King and others of the RCMP who participated in the chase, that Johnson reacted, not just at his cabin but with others he met during 1930 and '31, as if he thought the Mounties knew something about him that, in reality, they did not know. His absolute refusal to speak to them from their first, relatively minor question regarding trap lines, to his final shootout, seem to be the actions of a guilty man.

Nonetheless, when everything is added up and weighed, Johnson's connection with the Chicago crime world, while interesting, is solely conjecture, and perhaps paints a more ominous picture of the man than he deserves. The rifle John had with him at death was purchased at the Taylor & Drury store, not stolen. The money in his possession was not traced to a robbery or illicit trade of any kind. No revolver was found among his effects or secreted along a trail. As to his altered fingerprints, forty-five days on the trail making campfires without even the most primitive camp amenities could easily account for superficial burns or scarring of the fingertips.

Indeed, according to William Carter, the RCMP constable

who investigated the series of events that led to the shooting of King, Albert Johnson was innocent of the complaints brought against him. Carter questioned the Indians about snowshoe tracks of Johnson near their trap lines.[3] They said that they had seen none, but that their traps were set off and presumably furs were missing. Constable Carter stated that such creatures as owls, wolverines, and wolves sometimes pulled smaller animals out of traps, and so any of them could have been the "culprit". No furs were found in the Mad Trapper's possession.

In short, the probable cause for the complaint, when the personal politics of the situation are carefully analyzed, was the simple fact that Johnson had unwittingly plopped himself down amongst the trap lines of others, and there was understandable resentment. Here, where survival is a full-time preoccupation, territoriality is a powerful force.

My final thoughts on the subject are that Johnson, though he exhibited some of the characteristics, was never a killer per se and would not have been the Chicago hitman. I see him as a bull-headed man rejected by society, dogged by his own restlessness and sense of adventure, who sought to "go straight" in the northern wilderness, at the edge of the last frontier. He failed, not because of recidivism, but because of events—perhaps beyond his control—at Rat River that bore in on him and pushed him off a psychological cliff from whence there was no return. Like Butch Cassidy in his last redoubt, Johnson elected to shoot his inquisitors rather than talk to them, and that is where the string ran out.

ENDNOTES

PROLOGUE
1. Source is a paper by Mrs. A. B. Thornthwaite, wife of the RCMP Corporal who commanded the Old Crow detachment during the manhunt.
2. Anecdote related by Cliff Hagen, former Special Constable at Fort McPherson.
3. Letter from Edgar Millen to A. N. Eames, August 1, 1931.
4. Recollections of Mrs. A. B. Thornthwaite. 1932. Yukon Archives.
5. Later, Moses was so disturbed by what he had done that he threw his rifle away. He said he did not like the idea of eating meat that had been shot with a gun that had killed a man.
6. Interview with the author at Kamloops, B.C., July, 1969.

CHAPTER 1
1. This reference was probably to one Harry Johnson, to be discussed in chapter 5.
2. *The Mad Trapper of Rat River* (Macmillan, 1972, 1976).
3. Based on interviews for first book.
4. See Appendix B for a more detailed physical description. (A dental description was also included as an appendix in my first book.)
5. To the writer's knowledge, there is no copy of the original magazine extant. I have in my possession a photocopy of the article, but it does not show exact date, volume number, or name of the magazine!
6. Terry Shaw, *RCMP Quarterly*, Fall, 1960.

CHAPTER 2
1. Johnson's use of the name "Pete" is not necessarily contradictory to

the memory of others. He used a plethora of aliases in his travels, as will become clearer later on.

CHAPTER 3

1. Detracting from this revelation is the fact that there was an Indian woodcutter of the same name at Dawson City at the time who could have made the trip.
2 See Chapter 5 of *The Mad Trapper of Rat River* which refers to Nelson's search for lost mines in the Mackenzie Mountains.

CHAPTER 4

1. *The Wind and the Caribou*, Eric Munsterhjelm. (London: Macmillan, 1976).
2. *The Silence of the North*, Olive Frederickson. (New York: Crown, 1972).

CHAPTER 5

1. *Juneau Daily Empire*, November 26, 1923, p. 8. United States Attorney's office quoted pertaining to Johnson's service with the Mounted Police.
2. The name has been changed to protect living relatives.
3. "Trapping the Mad Trapper of Rat River", W. R. May, *True Detective Mysteries Magazine*, Oct./Nov., 1932.
4. Metzner's name was misspelled "Metzker" in Luke May's article.
5. See Appendix A—Personal Effects of Albert Johnson.

CHAPTER 7

1. *The Town That Got Lost*, Robert Loudon. (Gray's Publishing, Sydney, B.C., 1973).

CHAPTER 9

1. In North America, he adopted the name "Andrew Johnson".
2. Rustad, in his essay, presented another version. He said Johnny donned female attire, and boarded a train at Bainville to make his escape, but I could not verify this episode.

CHAPTER 10

1. The criminal information sheet dated March 20, 1915, shows "*The State of Wyoming v. Peterson*". The name "Peterson" is then scratched out and replaced by "William Hoffner" as defendant.

The use of multiple aliases, first learned from Delker, must now have been an established trait.

2. By strange coincidence, Cassidy's former attorney, Douglas Preston, was Attorney General of the state of Wyoming when Johnny went to jail in 1915. See *Butch Cassidy, My Brother* by Lula Parker Betenson, Brigham University Press, 1975.

3. He later sent her a gold watch from Wyoming. Thora, however, married another farmer, and they never saw each other again.

4. Recall the shoot-out alluded to in the Foreword: according to news sources in La Paz, Bolivia, the gun battle was touched off when an army lieutenant queried Cassidy and Longabough about a mule in their possession with an army brand on it. When the investigator persisted, the two men answered with their guns, killing the officer, and initiating the shoot-out in which they would die.

Completing the analogy between Cassidy and Johnson, the Mounties who killed the latter found a solitary cartridge stuffed in the butt of his rifle, giving him the morbid option of not being taken alive.

CHAPTER 11

1. Second-guessing a man's modus operandi and then employing it in a search is often an underestimated research method. Learning of Johnson's arrest in California, I suspected that he would likely have been resident in an area known for ranching and wilderness, so I had written to the courts of California's three northeastern counties, one being Lassen. On the first go-round, I missed him because he had been booked under an alias, but he was indeed arrested in one of the three counties I predicted he would have been in.

2. It may be more than coincidence that Harvey Logan (aka "Kid" Curry) of the Wild Bunch was using the alias Charles W. Johnson when he was arrested in Knoxville, Tennessee in 1901.

3. Letter from Dr. William F. Davis, Kingsville, Ohio, June 20, 1974. Davis discussed the appraisal made by a friend of his who is a psychiatrist. (Another theory is that Johnson was waiting for it to snow so his tracks would be covered when he fled).

CHAPTER 12

1. See below, this chapter, for explanation of fingerprint terminology.

2. A system of identification that predated the fingerprint method which replaced it.
3. In fact, the very recent discovery of ways to use DNA analysis for identification may invalidate this claim.

CHAPTER 14

1. Quoted from *True Detective Mysteries Magazine*, October/ November, 1932.
2. William Carter in a letter to the author, 1971.
3. The councillors also supposed that they represented the community, and were somewhat disturbed by the Minister's decision. They dispatched a brusque letter to him stating as much.

EPILOGUE

1. Republished as *Jake Lingle: Or Chicago on the Spot*, John Boettiger. (New York: Dutton, 1931).
2. A left-handed glove was also found discarded at the scene indicating the murderer was left-handed. Johnny Johnson, it must be remembered, could shoot with either hand.
3. Letter to the author from Carter, April 18, 1970.
4. According to interviews with Angie Johnson, Johnny's niece, and other surviving relatives.
5. In addition to my first book on the Mad Trapper, a book called *The Lost Patrol* (Anchorage: Alaska North-West Pub. Co., 1978) about four Mounties on the Dawson–Ft-McPherson patrol in 1911 who got lost and starved to death.
6. Ex-Supt. Chris Tiller claims to have seen the prints as late as 1960 or thereabouts. I have not been able to ascertain who might have given the order to destroy them since then.

PERSONAL EFFECTS OF ALBERT JOHNSON

Small glass bottle containing:
five pearls, approximate value $15.00 and five pieces of gold dental
   work 4 dwt. approximate value $3.20

Small glass bottle containing:
13 dwt. of alluvial gold, approximate value $9.36. *Articles which it is
   requested be left with the Royal Canadian Mounted Police for inclusion in
   the Royal Canadian Mounted Police Museum at Regina, Sask.*
Savage 30-30 Rifle, No. 293575, Model 99.
Iver Johnson Sawed off shot gun, No. 5537XF. 16 ga.
.22 Winchester Rifle, Model 58, No number. Stock sawn off.
Pocket Compass.
Axe—Handle bearing bullet mark.
Sack containing lard tin and lid used as tea pail, showing bullet holes.
Articles of no value, for which authority to destroy is requested.
Knife made from spring trap.
Match safe.
Gillette Safety Razor.
Envelope containing piece of three cornered file; awl made from three
   cornered file; chisel made from nail.
Small knife made from piece of metal, with mooseskin cover.
Mooseskin Rifle cover.
Mooseskin pouch.
Mooseskin sewing pouch containing needles and thread.
Small spring.
Nails wrapped in tinfoil.
Matches wrapped in tinfoil.

30-30 Cartridge box containing small empty bottle and pieces of wax.

Sack containing thirty-nine 30-30 shells.

   1 box .22 shells (30)

   1 box .22 shells (30)

Seven pieces of moosehide.

Sack containing six empty sacks;

   15 pieces of babiche.

    1 large bundle of babiche. (snowshoe lacing)

    1 bdle. Sewing thread.

    1 piece mooseskin lace.

Calico rifle cover.

Large envelope containing:

1 box Pony Matches.

1 bndl Sulphur Matches wrapped in tinfoil.

1 bndl Sulphur Matches wrapped in paper.

1 tinfoil packet containing 2 pills.

1 paper package containing six pills.

1 paper package containing fish hooks.

1 tinfoil package containing oily rag.

1 leather cover containing comb and sewing materials.

1 paper and tinfoil package containing grey powder.

1 rag bundle containing twine.

1 rag bundle containing sewing twine.

1 paper package containing 24 pills.

1 paper package containing fish hooks.

4 .22 shells

4 – 16 ga. Shot Gun Shells.

1 Moosehide folder containing mirror.

1 rag containing pepper.

1 sack containing salt.

VITAL STATISTICS AND MODUS OPERANDI

Albert Johnson

1. Hair
   a) Light brown
   b) Part on the left
   c) Evidence of a cowlick

   d) Tuft, back of head

   e) Condition—Mussed up from hat and continual sweating, and freezing
   f) Beard—Light brown

2. Forehead
   a) Receding

3. Head
   a) Length—Not known

   b) Width—Not known

John K. Johnson

1. Hair
   a) Light chestnut
   b) Part on the left
   c) Cowlick (Wyoming photo)
   d) Tuft, back of head (Wyoming photo)
   e) Combed

   f) Beard—Light brown

2. Forehead
   a) Receding (San Quentin)
   b) Low

3. Head
   a) Length—19 cm or 7.48 inches
   b) Width—15.2 cm or 5.98 inches (Bertillon measurements, San Quentin)

Albert Johnson	**John K. Johnson**
4. Ears (from front)	4. Ears (from front, San Quentin)
a) Left ear protrudes	a) Left ear protrudes
b) Right ear close to head	b) Right ear close to head
5. Left ear	5. Left Ear
a) Disfigured lobe from frostbite or injury	a) Normal
b) Length—not known	b) Length—5.7 cm or 2.24 inches
6. Right ear	6. Right ear
a) Start of helix rim	a) Exact similarity to Albert's
b) Anti-helix	b) Similar
c) Concha	c) Similar
d) Anti-tragus	d) Similar
e) Minute creases upper portion of Helix Rim	e) Exact similarity to Albert's
f) Tragus—slightly forked	f) Tragus—not forked
g) Lobule (flesh lines)	g) Lobule—lower portion does not compare favourably with Albert's

Note: Ear expert A. V. Iannarelli says difference of the tragus and lobule could be due to frostbite, dehydration, and the camera angle

7. Cheekbones—Prominent	7. Cheekbones—Prominent

8. Supraorbital ridges above eyes of both men are similar (Dr. J. V. Clark)

9. Face—no outstanding marks, moles, or scars	9. Face—no outstanding marks, moles, or scars

10. Teeth—poor, but well cared for (Dr. Urquhart) Dental chart	10. Teeth—poor (San Quentin, though no dental chart)
11. Lips—thin. Upper—prognathic	11. Lips—thin. Upper—prognathic
12. Chin a) Evidence of cleft b) Appearance—jutting. Caused by beard and camera angle (Dr. J. V. Clark)	12. Chin a) Cleft visible b) Receding
13. Mouth—medium	13. Mouth—medium
14. Eyes a) Light blue b) Heavy lids	14. Eyes a) Blue b) Left eye injured with a bull whip when young (Gladys Weirson Hansen. Montana records call it a "cataract". Injury evident in photos) c) Heavy lids
15. Nose—Swollen from frostbite a) Ridge—convex b) Length—short (probably due to camera angle, Dr. J. V. Clark) c) Roots—deep ("flaring" nostrils) d) Nostril—Right slightly larger than left (Death photo)	15. Nose—normal a) Ridge—convex b) Length—medium (San Quentin) c) Roots—Deep (San Quentin) d) Nostril—Right slightly larger than left (Montana, though may be due to camera angle)

Albert Johnson	**John K. Johnson**
e) Base—normal. Breadth—medium	e) Base—normal. Breadth—medium
	f) Projection—"Pr" (San Quentin symbol)
16. Arms Exceptionally long. (Observation, Wop May, *True Detective Mysteries Magazine*, 1932)	16. Arms Long (from San Quentin measurements). Outstretched (Bertillon method)—1 m 77 cms or 69.68 inches, or .48 inches longer than his height
17. Shoulders Right shoulder lower than his left (though mostly covered by a canvas in death photo, close examination of right deltoid appears to confirm this)	17. Shoulders Right obviously lower than left (See Wyoming and San Quentin photos)
18. Fingers Length—not known	18. Fingers Length—long. Middle finger, 12.2 cm or 4.8 inches. (Bertillon method from the knuckle). Little finger, 9.8 cm or 3.86 inches in length from the knuckle to the tip
19. Forearms—not known	19. Forearm—47.3 cm or 18.62 inches (San Quentin)
20. Feet Length—9½ inches (Approximate, Dr. J. A. Urquhart's measurement	20. Feet Length—Left—27.0 cm or 10.63 inches (Bertillon method of measurement

made after death with no weight on arch also possibly affected by dehydration and starvation)

dictates that the individual being measured must balance all his weight on the foot being measured with the other foot in the air so that the full weight falls on the arch)

21. Trunk
    Length—not known

21. Trunk
    Length—93.5 cm or 36.81 inches (San Quentin)

22. Height—5 feet nine to five feet nine and one-half inches (estimated by Dr. Urquhart)

22. Height—5 feet nine and one-quarter inches, or 1 meter 75.8 cm (San Quentin)

23. Build—Rugged

23. Build—Muscular (San Quentin)

24. Complexion—not known

24. Complexion—Fair (San Quentin)
    Light—Florid (Wyoming)

25. Age—At death estimated to be between 35 and 40

25. Age—If Johnny were Albert, he would have been 33 years seven months at death on February 17, 1932. DOB July 13, 1898, in Bardu, Norway

Fingerprints and Identifying Marks

Albert Johnson

John K. Johnson

1. Fingers
   a) Left forefinger—Radial Loop.

1. Fingers
   a) Right forefinger—Radial Loop.

Albert Johnson	John K. Johnson
b) Left middle finger— Ulnar loop. (Only record available is a memo referring to the above named patterns. Neither fingerprint card nor classification can be located in RCMP records.)	b) Right middle finger— Ulnar Loop.
	c) Left forefinger— Whorl.
	d) Left middle finger— Whorl.
	Odds against right forefingers being radial loops are five to one.
Odds against left forefingers being radial loops are six to one.	Odds on right middle fingers being ulnar loops are a little better than one in two.
Odds on left middle fingers being ulnar loops are a little better than one in two.	Classification: Right—11 R I0 19 Left—4-00 17

(Figures based on percentage frequency of occurrence of pattern types by finger, RCMP records comprising 1.4 million subjects.)

2. Scars, Marks, Etc.	2. Scars, Marks, Etc.
a) No circumcision scar.	a) No circumcision scar.
b) No vaccination scar.	b) No vaccination scar.
c) No operation scars of any sort (Dr. J. A. Urquhart's examination).	c) No operation scars are reported on physical examination forms in three prisons (Wyoming, Montana, and California).
d) Ordinary scars (Dr. Urquhart omitted any reference to scars other than "operation" scars).	d) Ordinary non-operational scars. a) Spot scar left elbow joint.

e) Mole two inches to the left of spine in mid lumbar region.

b) Large cut scar lower left leg.

c) Dim scar left palm.

e) Large brown birthmark on median link centre of back.

f) Small mole under right nipple (reported at Montana, but not California or Wyoming).

Modus Operandi

Albert Johnson

1. Trader Roy Buttle stated that the man he figured was Albert Johnson (Arthur Nelson, Dick Johnson, etc.) told him he was "raised on a farm in North Dakota". Buttle met this man at the Ross River, Yukon Territory store of Taylor and Drury in late summer, 1927.

2 "Johnson was a cowboy." Words of the late Tom Sturgeon, RCMP Constable at Whitehorse and Teslin in the late twenties.

3. Spoke with a slight Scandinavian accent (newspaper, RCMP reports re: Albert Johnson).

John K. Johnson

1. Was raised on a farm near the community of Gladys, township of Climax, Williams County, North Dakota. Left his relatives in spring, 1923 and headed north into Canada. Never heard from again.

2. Broke horses and herded cattle while living at his father's farm. Source: Williams County History.

3. Born in Bardu, Norway, of a Swedish father and Norwegian mother. Neither parent ever learned English (see Bardu baptismal certificate and Williams County History). Emi-

Albert Johnson	John K. Johnson
	grated to the United States with his family in 1904, at age of six (Williams County Court Records).
4. Loner (RCMP reports)	4. When arrested by the law, both times he was alone (see Lincoln County, Wyoming, Court Records, and Lassen County, California, Court Records).
5. Outdoor man. Investigated regarding a trap line dispute. RCMP chased him through the wilderness for almost two months.	5. Outdoor man. Robbed bank and got away on horseback. Brother caught, but John escaped. Went hunting and trapping wolves in what is now the Green River National Forest in Wyoming.
6. Did not carry identification (see RCMP reports).	6. No identification on his person when arrested in Wyoming and California (see court records).
7. Use of aliases. Albert Johnson and possibly Arthur Nelson, Dick Johnson.	7. Use of aliases, William Hoffner, Charles W. Johnson, and possibly "Peterson" (see prison records: San Quentin, and Wyoming, Lincoln County jails).
8. Clothes—When killed by RCMP he was wearing overalls with a bib (report	8. Clothes—When arrested by Wyoming authorities he was wearing overalls with

of Corp. Thornthwaite
NCO–in–charge, Old
Crow, Yukon Territory).

a bib (see Wyoming prison
photos).

9. Propensity to lie when
occasion demanded it (see
R.C.M.P. Quarterly, 1960).

9. Consistently fibbed about
name, age, and origin (see
prison records, Wyoming,
Montana. Also court rec-
ords Lassen County, Cali-
fornia, and Lincoln
County, Wyoming.

10. Propensity to steal when
occasion arose.

10. Arrested for stealing on
three different occasions
(see court records).

11. Tendency to double back
when chased (see RCMP
reports, R. C. Signals
reports).

11. Doubled back when
tracked in California (see
testimony of tracker Isaac
Baughman, Preliminary
Hearing, *State vs. Charles
W. Johnson*).

12. Willingness to resort to
the use of firearms. Shot
Const. King, Sergt. Her-
sey, and killed Const.
Millen. Excellent shot (see
RCMP records). Could fire
two pistols simultaneously
from a cross-handed posi-
tion.

12. Used guns in hold-up of
Von Eschen, Haefner
Hardware store in Bain-
ville, Montana; Farmers'
State Bank, in Medicine
Lake, Montana; and shot
his way through a posse to
escape after the bank hold-
up. Excellent shot (see
newspapers such as *Medi-
cine Lake Wave*, February/
March, 1915). Could
shoot a pistol from under
a horse's neck at full gallop.

APPENDIX C

SOURCES

Newspapers

Alaska
Juneau Daily Empire—for 1923: June 30; July 7, 30; September 2, 3, 24, 25, 26, 28, 30; November 26, 30; December 1, 6.
Stroller's Weekly—for 1923: September 30; December 1.

California
Lassen County Advocate—for 1921: May 27; July 15, 22; August 12.

Idaho
Idaho Falls Register—for 1916: March 28.
Rexburg Current Journal—for 1916: March 31.
Idaho Falls Times—for 1916: March 30.

Montana
Medicine Lake Wave—for 1915: February 11, 19, 25; March 11.
Plentywood Herald—for 1915: February 12; March 19; October 8; November 5. For 1916: August 16, 25.
The Searchlight and *Culbertson Republican*—for 1915: February 12, 19; April 2. For 1916: March 26; August 11; September 29.
Sheridan County News—for 1915: February 13; June 18.

North Dakota
Bismarck Tribune—for 1915: February 18.
Williston Herald—for 1915: February 18, 25; March 4. For 1916: October 4.

Wyoming
Kemmerer Camera—for 1915: March 24; May 26, 29; June 2.

Yukon Territory
Dawson City News—for 1930: August 7.

Court Papers

Melville Judicial District of the Province of Saskatchewan—*His Majesty the King vs. Harry Johnson*, September 10, 1920.

Seventeenth Judicial District of the State of Montana, Plentywood, Sheridan County—*The State of Montana vs. John Johnson*, August 5, 1916.

Third Judicial District of the State of Wyoming, Kemmerer, Lincoln County—*The State of Wyoming vs. William Hoffner*, March 20, 1915.

Superior Court, Lassen County, Susanville, California—*State of California vs. Charles W. Johnson*, June 8, 1921.

Historical Societies and Archives

Alberta Provincial Archives
California Historical Society
California State Archives
Idaho Historical Society
Lassen County Historical Society
Montana Historical Society
National Archives of Canada
North Dakota Historical Society
Saskatchewan Provincial Archives
Wyoming Historical Society
Wyoming State Archives
Yukon Archives

Jail Records

Folsom Prison
Idaho State Penitentiary
Lincoln County Jail
McNeil Island Penitentiary
Montana State Penitentiary
San Quentin Penitentiary
Wyoming State Penitentiary

List of Persons Interviewed

In addition to those listed in the Index, the following persons were interviewed for background information:

Robin Armour, *Whitehorse, Yukon*
Bob Cameron, *Whitehorse, Yukon*
Bette Clark, *Toronto, Ontario*
Dave Clemetson, *Gladys, N. Dakota*
Anjeunette Cory, *Toronto, Ontario*
Everett Crusch, *Bainville, Montana*
Diane Dayton, *Kemmerer, Wyoming*
Willy De Wolfe, *Dawson City, Yukon*
Johan Flekstad, *Bardu, Norway*
Gordon & Blanche Hansen, *Olds, Alberta*
Turid Hevde, *Sondefjord, Norway*
Maud von Eschen Hilton, *Bainville, Montana*
Robert La Pointe, *Juneau, Alaska*
Nancy Marron, *Plentywood, Montana*
Angie McCarvel, *Medicine Lake, Montana*
Bob McLeod, *Kemmerer, Wyoming*
Robert Olsen, *Burlingame, Kansas*
Bonnie Pacovsky, *Bainville, Montana*
Mike Prieto, *Rochester, New York*
Tim Purdy, *Susanville, California*
Terry Shaw, *Ottawa, Ontario*
Chris Tiller, *Ottawa, Ontario*
Ed Vanetta, *Bainville, Montana*
Malcolm Wake, *Regina, Saskatchewan*
John Woltz, *Helena, Montana*

INDEX

(Entries in italic indicate photographs)

Abbott, Thomas, 52-4
Acland, Superintendent A. C.,
    7-9
Adjutant General, N. Dakota,
    29-30
Aklavik, N.W.T., ix, 5-7, 9, 12,
    16, 17, 21, 45, 132, 165-6
Alaska, 8, 20, 64-5, 74, 161,
    175-6
Alaska State Troopers, 26-7,
    161
Alcatraz Prison, xi, 67
Alexie, Peter, 10, 18, 45
Alexie, Robert, 45-7
Anchorage, Alaska, 8
Anderson, Bill, 85-6
Anderson, H. G., 100
Andre, James, 153
Anyox, British Columbia,
    78-83
Arctic Red River, 4
Arey, Tom, (Mayor), 165
Asp, Ed, 26-7, 72, 138
Atkinson, W. H. "Billy", 43

Bainville, Montana, 98-102,
    112-13
Bangs, Andy, 95-6
Banty, "Coyote" Bill, 68, *69*,
    70-72

Barrier River, 10
Baughman, Isaac Henry,
    119-21
Bauman, Katherine, 92
Beckman, Milo, 71-2
Bell River, 11, 85-6
Benson, Mr., Mrs. A. C., 56,
    57, *58*, 59
Bergman Hotel, 65
Bernard, Joe, 4, 5
Betenson, Lula Parker, 181
Bibber, Alex Van, 21
Biederman, Alex, 176-7
Black Lake, Sask., xi, 59-63
Blake, Arthur, 4
Boettiger, John, 182
Bolivia, ix
Bowen, Jack, 9
Branstrom, Phil, 85-6, *87*
Breckinridge, Wilbur, 68-70
British Columbia, mining, *see*
    Anyox, Yukon
Brookshore, Clay, 161
Brothers, Leo V., 175, *176*
Brown, John Barkauckas, 18
"Butch Cassidy" (Robert Leroy
    Parker), x, 98, 109-115, 178,
    181
Buttle, Roy, 28, 32, 81
Byerhof, Joe, 73-4

California, 77, 117–122
Capital Hotel, Yukon, 20
Capone, Al, 175
Carmacks, Yukon, 33, 43–4
Carrière, Roxie (Trading Post), 44
Carter, Constable William, 9–10, 177–8, 182
Chesterton, Reverend, 166
Chicago, Illinois, x, xi, 52–4, 175
Chicago *Tribune*, x, 52, 174
Church, Sheriff J. S., 119–121
Chute Pass, 3
Clark, Dr. J. V., 129–30
Clark, George, 85–6
Coleman, Tom, 59–62
Cooper, Don, 160–5
Coppermine, N.W.T., 18
Craft, Dick, 64–5, 153
Craft, Katie, 64–7
Creedon, Dan, 108–9
Crooked Creek, Yukon, 37

Davis, Dr. William F., 181
Dawson City News, 42, 52, *53*, 176
Dawson City, Yukon, 36–9, 42–7, 50–2, 177
Dawson, Malcolm, 160
Dease Lake, B.C., 27–8, 72, 77, 138
Delker, Bert (Marinus B. Mortenson), 98–9
Dept. of Vital Statistics, N.W.T., 131–2
Devaney, Corporal M. R., 60
Dixon, Rev. Geoffrey, 132
Douglas, Bill (Trading Post), 44

Duggan, Sheriff John, 101–6
Dunleavy, Corporal Patrick, 26, 168–9
Dyck, Corporal Ray, 60
Dyer, Bruce, 117

Eagle, Alaska, 51, 174
Eagle River, Yukon, 11, 16, 24, 85–6
Eames, Inspector A. N., 5–12, 16–20, 24
Edmonton, Alberta, 7, 8, 19
Eide, Marlene, 116

Farmers' State Bank, Medicine Lake, Montana, 100, *101*, 102–3
Field, Poole, 33
Fink, Mike, 112–13
Folsom Prison, 121, *122*
Folvag, Julian, 136–142
Fort McPherson, N.W.T., 1–4, 7, 17–19, 24–6, 44, 50, 85, 152–4
Fort Selkirk, Yukon, 35–7, 42
Fort Smith, N.W.T., 62–3
Fox, Lilly, 149–50
Frances, Abe, 2, *3*, 44–5
Frederickson, Olive, 62–3, 180
Fur, Fish and Game Magazine, 73–4

Geddes, Reverend, 24
Gill, R. J., 19
Godfrey, Det. Sgt. Ralph H., 163–4
Green, Alec, 167
Grey, Loren, 77
Grey, Romer, 77
Grey, Zane, xi, 74–7

Grossgard, Sheriff, 101
Guder, Fritz, 33-4
Gull, Joe, 69-72

Haefner, Louis (Hardware
   Store), 100, 108
Hagen, Cliff, 179
Hansen, Knute, 165
Haug, Martin, 133
Haug, Oscar, 133, 136-8
Hebb, Chief Coroner Sheldon,
   164
Hejde, Mrs. Hannah, 98-9
Henry, Annie, 39
Henry, Joe, 38-9, 51
Hermanson, Thora, 99
Hersey, Sgt. Earl, 11, 12, 45
Hickey, Mrs. Vicky, 164
Hickman, Dick (Editor, *North
   Dakota Peace Officers'
   Journal*), 155, 172
"Hoffner, William", 107-109,
   110, 180; *see also* Johnson,
   Johnny
Holm, Henry, 18
Hudson's Bay Company
   (Trading Post, Fort
   McPherson), 2
Hutchings, Ozzie, 81-3

Iannarelli, A. V., 130
Idaho State, xi, 43, 68-71
Inuvik, N.W.T., 85

Jack, Scambella, 43-4
Jackson Brothers' Trading Post,
   10-12
James, Chief Coroner R. L.,
   133-6, 162
Jasmin, Sask., 64

Jenson, Pete, 21
John, Arthur, 21, 41-4, 125,
   153-5
Johnny, Lonnie, 21, 43
Johnson, Albert (the "Mad
   Trapper"), ix, *x*, xi; at Fort
   McPherson, 1-4; siege of
   Johnson's cabin, 5-8; chase
   by posse, 6-12; killing of
   Const. Millen, 8; final shoot-
   out on Eagle River, 11-12;
   physical description, 1, 7,
   24-6, 34, 55-6, 68, 126-38,
   149-55, 168, *169*, *171*, 174;
   personality and habits, 1-10,
   24-9, 52-5, 122-3, 172;
   firearms expertise, 1, 2, 7-9,
   24-5, 74; fingerprints, 9, 16,
   131, 136, 139, 142-8,
   161-8; *see also* Johnson,
   Johnny
Johnson, Angie, 182
Johnson, Bill, 57, *58*, 59, 63
"Johnson, Charles W.", 117, *118*,
   121; *see also* Johnson, Johnny
Johnson, "Deep Hole", 18
Johnson, Dick, 42-3, 56, 176
Johnson, Harry, 64-5, *66*, 67,
   179
Johnson, Johnny (born Johan
   Konrad Jonsen, aka Albert
   Johnson, Arthur Nelson,
   Charles W. Johnson, William
   Hoffner), 92; childhood,
   93-97; robberies and
   rustling, 100-02, 111-12,
   117-21; physical description,
   124-30, 133, 136-8,
   149-59, 168, *170*, 171-4;
   personality and habits,

99-107, 114, 119-23, 156,
172; firearms expertise,
97-9, 102, 159; fingerprints,
125, 136-9, 142-6, *147*, 148
Johnson, Mrs. Obert, 116
Johnson, Sharon, 116-17
Jonson, Anders "Andrew"
Gustaf, 93-5, 110, 137
Jonson, Helga, 93, 111, 116,
137
Jonson, Magnor Hansen, 92-3,
99-103, 109, 137
Jonson, Olga, 94, 116, 137
Jonson, Petra, 93-5, 130, 133,
137
Jonson, Signe, 94, 99, 137
Juneau, Alaska, 42, 65, 74,
161
Juneau Daily Empire, 42, 180

Keen, Chuck, 20
Kemmerer *Camera* (Wyoming),
108
Keno City, Yukon, 21, 45-8
"Kid Curry" (Harvey Logan),
98, 181
King, Constable Alfred, 4-6,
45, 167, 177
Kitchen, Sam, 84-6
Klondike River, 37-8
Krom, Joe E., 19
Kromona Mining and Smelting
Company (Spokane,
Washington), 19
Kulan, Al, 21

Ladue, Jack, 21, 43
Ladue, Joe, 21, 43
Lang, Knut, 6-8
Lansing, Yukon, 43
La Pierre House, Yukon, 3, 11,

12, 154-5
Lassen County, California, 117
Lincoln County Jail, Wyoming,
107, 124-25
Lindsay, Virginia, 32
Lingle, Alfred "Jake", xi, 52-4,
174-5
Logan, Harvey, *see* "Kid Curry"
Long, Goddard, 117-121
Longabaugh, Harry, *see*
"Sundance Kid"
"Lost" Mines, rumours, 74-77
Loudon, Robert, 81, 180

Mackenzie River, N.W.T., 3, 4,
8, 18, 24
"Mad Trapper", *see* Johnson,
Albert
Marion, Joe, 59, 63
Martin, Dr. J. D., 132
Martin, John, *35*, 38-45, 50-1
Martin, Richard, 50-1, 174
Martin, Robert (Special
Constable), 21, 38, 43, 67
May, Detective Luke, 68-71,
180
May, Constable Sid, 9-12
May, W. R. "Wop", 9-12, 67-8,
163, 180
Mayo, Yukon, 21, 41-3, 47-8
McNevin, Jack, 61
McQuesten River, Yukon, 45-8
Medicine Lake, Montana, 100,
101-103
Medicine Lake *Wave*, 104, *105*
Meloy, Jack, 36-8
Meloy, Mrs., 38
Mervyn, James, 43
Mervyn, Norman, 43
Mexico, xi, 74-7
Middle Lake, Sask., 59-61

Millen, Constable Edgar, 3-8, 19, 24, 28, 179
Miller, Cal, 20-21
Minook, Alberta, 16
Missouri River, 96, 102, 112-14
Moi, Laura Sullivan, 156-58
Montana, 18-19, 98-114
Montana State Penitentiary, 98, 107-09, 125, 137-43
Moses, Special Constable John, 9-11, 179
"Mounties", *see* Royal Canadian Mounted Police
Mullet, Harry F., 28
Munden, Dolores, 108
Munsterhjelm, Erik, 57-63, 180

Nation, Alaska, 19
"Nelson, Arthur", 27-34, *35*, 36-50, 55-6, 78, 138, 150; *see also* Johnson, Johnny
Nelson, Nels, 62-3
Nerysoo, William, 4
New Sweden Irrigation Project, 69-72
Nielson, Sivert, 74-5, *76*, 77
Nieman, Paul, 24, 86, 125, 154-5
North Dakota, 28-30, 81, 92-97
North Dakota State Historical Society, 30-1, 92
Northern Trader's Store, 2, 153, 176-7
Northwest Territories, Canada, 1-4, 152, 160
Norway, 94-5

Old Crow, Yukon, 9, 18

O'Neil, Barry, 21
Ostenstad, Ole, 45-9

Parker, Robert Leroy, *see* "Butch Cassidy"
Peel River, 1-4, 8
Pelly River, 36-7
Peter, George, 43
Petersen, Victor, 18
"Peterson, Pete" (aka Anderson), 59-63, 73-4, 79-80, 173
Pinkerton Detective Agency, 107
Plentywood *Herald* (Montana), 104-07
Poling, Hyder, 96
Preston, Douglas (Attorney General, Wyoming), 181

Rat River, 4-11, 45, 85-6
R.C.M.P., *see* Royal Canadian Mounted Police
RCMP Quarterly, 28, 34, 166, 179
Richardson Mountains, Yukon, 8-10, 156
Riddell, Frank, 45
Risbie, Peter, 41
Robert, John, 2, 44, 125, 152-55
Ross River, 21, 28-50, 55, 153
Royal Canadian Mounted Police, xi; the hunt for Johnson, 3-16; rumours of Johnson's identity, 16-26, 41, 60, 64, 67-8, 84-5, 116, 133-39, 146, 177
Royal Northwest Mounted Police, 64
Rustad, Wallace, 92-100, 107, 130-33, 180

San Quentin Penitentiary, California, 116, 121, 127
Saskatchewan, xi, 57-60, 64, 116
Seattle *Times*, 103
Seeberg, Elizabeth, 77
Shaw, Terry, 179
Sheridan County, N. Dakota, 103-04, 125
Sierra Packing Company, California, 119-20
Slim, Frank, 32-37, 42-3, 55
Smith, Tom, 125, 149-155
Snowbird Lake, 61
Spare, John, 29
Sperry, Bishop John, 132
Stanley, Lena, 155-6, *157*, 158-9
Stepan, John Sylvester, 16-17
Sterriah, Paul, 43-4
Stewart River, 21, 37, 43-48
Stoney Rapids, Sask., 57-63
Sturgeon, Tom, 92
"Sundance Kid", the, (Harry Longabaugh), x, 181
Susanville, California, 117-121

Taylor and Drury Supply Warehouse, 28, 33, 177
Taylor, J. M., 19
Terry, Lorne, 61
Teslin Lake, B.C., 28, 36
Thornthwaite, Corporal Arthur B., 9
Thornthwaite, Mrs., 179
Tiller, Chris, 182
Troy, Montana, 18-19
True Detective Mysteries Magazine, 67, *69*, 180-82

Urquhart, Coroner J. A., 25, 51, 55, 126-9

Van Bibber, George, 41
Van Bibber, Mrs., 39-40
Vancouver, B.C., 57-8
Vancouver *Sun*, 56, *58*-9
Veres, Corporal Nick, 43-4
Verville, Joe, 12

Watson, W. W., 136-9, 147-8
Weirson, Johnny, 116, 137
Weiss, Hilda, 65-6
Wernecke Mountains, Yukon, 21, 48
Whitehorse, Yukon, 23, 32-38
"Wild Bunch", the, *see* "Butch Cassidy"
Williams County, N. Dakota, 92, 96, 103, 137
Wilson, Janet, 160
Wood, Inspector, S. T., 17-18
Wyoming State, 99, 107-12, 124
Wyoming State Penitentiary, 110, 111, 126, 173

Yukon Indian News, 160
Yukon River, 23, 36, 174
Yukon Rose (riverboat), 36-7, 43, 176
Yukon Territory, 4, 18-20, 32-42, 47-51; climate, terrain, 10, 18-23, 33-9, 42, 47-51, 151-2; "lost" mines, 20-21, 37, 47, 50

Zaruba, Tom, 161-3
Zawrocha, Corporal Ed, 43